WHEN I'M 64

Planning For the ~~Rest~~ *Best* of Your Life

MARVIN TOLKIN

AND

HOWARD MASSEY

TRIBUTARY
PRESS

New York

Dedicated to my beloved family, past and present

TRIBUTARY
PRESS

Tributary Press LLC
132 East 35th Street
Suite 8C
New York, NY 10016

Visit our website at www.tributarypress.com

Printed in the United States of America

First Printing: May 2009

ISBN-13 978-0-9824566-0-6

Library of Congress Control Number: 2009903709

WHEN I'M 64

Planning For the ~~Rest~~ *Best*
of Your Life

To Miriam —
Thanks for your input!
With best wishes

TABLE OF CONTENTS

FOREWORD
by Dr. Robert N. Butler

ONE OF THE MOST REMARKABLE ACHIEVEMENTS of mankind is the fact that, through medical advances and other technology, we have gained more than 50 years of life. Even more remarkable is that 30 of those extra years were gained in the twentieth century alone, greater than had been achieved during the preceding 5,000 years of human history combined.

It's clear, then, that most of us will live longer, and in better health, than our parents and grandparents. On the face of it, that's a wonderful thing; life, after all, is precious.

But what happens if you don't have the resources to enjoy those extra years?

Sadly, that's the question facing millions of people today.

Americans—especially the baby boomer generation about to enter their retirement years—are not good savers, and so they will have to do better in investing and work longer in order to avoid outliving their resources. Without significant planning, it will be impossible for them to support themselves during their two, three, or even four decades of retirement.

I founded the International Longevity Center in order to confront the dramatic changes in population longevity. From the outset, one of our main goals was to help convince baby boomers that they need to be interested in health promotion and disease prevention now, before it's too late. But just as important is the immediate need to become interested in financial planning and to begin nurturing your passions so that you can spend your retirement years in ways that are personally fulfilling, without money worries hanging over you like a virtual Sword of Damocles.

That's what *When I'm 64: Planning for the Best of Your Life* is all about. The interweaving of Marvin Tolkin's life story—a true success story—with folksy wisdom, practical advice, and incisive commentary is a powerful combination. Every baby boomer—and their children—should read this book.

My life's work is based on the premise of productive aging: the idea that even older people should continue to contribute to society, through civic engagement and other meaningful activities. Within these pages you'll find a toolkit of ideas that enables the construction of a foundation strong enough to support even the longest and most active of retirements.

Life, I have learned, has to be based on hope and the expectation of a positive future. This inspirational book provides both in abundance.

—Dr. Robert N. Butler
President and CEO,
International Longevity Center

INTRODUCTION

THE BEST IS
YET TO COME

THERE ARE LOTS OF "GET-RICH-QUICK" books out there that promise to tell you how to amass a fortune beyond your wildest dreams.

This isn't one of them.

There are other books that offer complex formulas for financial success, blueprints for making a killing in the stock market, or advice for assembling an investment portfolio that can't lose.

Sorry, this isn't one of them either.

This isn't even a retirement planning book per se. It's a *life* planning book. Its purpose is to answer one simple question: Once you reach that magic age of 64 (give or take a few years) and you're no longer working, what are you going to do with the rest of your life?

Specifically, what are you going to do to make the last third of your life the *best* third of your life?

My goal is to help you answer that question, and all the other questions that go with it. Questions like: How can you accumulate enough assets to allow you to live a comfortable lifestyle after you are no longer earning an income? How can you use your retirement years most productively? And, most importantly, how can you stack the odds in your favor in terms of maintaining both physical and mental health?

By now, you're probably asking yourself, "What makes this guy qualified to offer this kind of advice?" To be sure, I don't have any kind of formal degree or diploma that makes me an "official" Retirement Planner, Financial Planner, or any other kind of Planner.

But what I can proudly claim is a lifetime of study in the School Of Life.

You see, I'm 82 years young. I retired more than a decade ago, and with the benefit of a simple plan that my wife and I formulated when we were in our forties, I am currently enjoying the most wonderful, most fulfilling retirement anyone could wish for. You could say that I'm one lucky guy... but luck, as they say, is the residue of design.

Nonetheless, I have been blessed in so many ways. I have been blessed with good health and an insatiable curiosity for the world around me. I have been blessed with an unshakeable optimism, and through hard work and a little calculated risk, I have been blessed with financial success. Most of all, I have been blessed with family. I was raised by two loving, supportive parents who gave me a great start on life, and I've had three wonderful children who in turn have given me eight fantastic grandkids. Even tragedy has led to good fortune in that it's given me not just one great marriage, but two. (My first wife, Estelle, passed away suddenly and unexpectedly at the age of just 65;

serendipiditously, I met my second wife and current love of my life, Carole—who has given me three great stepchildren and five terrific grandkids—through the same man who introduced me to Estelle.)

In many ways, the last third of my life has indeed been the best third of my life. This book tells my story. It is my fervent hope that everyone reading these words will reap the benefits of my experience and be able to enjoy a retirement as satisfying and joyous as mine has been.

Of course, no one can do exactly what I did, because we're all individuals, with our own interests, goals, and dreams. But by following your passion, as I did, and by taking the time to do a little simple planning, you can enrich the last third of your life in ways that you may not even be able to imagine. It may sound trite or cliched, but armed with just a smattering of knowledge and a bit of luck, I can guarantee you that the best is yet to come.

—Marvin Tolkin

CHAPTER ONE

DEFINITELY NOT HEADED FOR BINGO NIGHT

"Too old to rock'n'roll, too young to die"
—*Jethro Tull*

THE SMALL METAL FAN WHIRRED OMINOUSLY in the background as my father shifted uncomfortably in his seat. It was a steamy afternoon in the summer of 1965 and he and I were sitting shoulder to shoulder in a modestly appointed office in midtown Manhattan. But it wasn't just the heat that was affecting my dad. It was the fact that he was being forced to make a decision that no father should ever have to make.

"There's no wiggle room, no time to hesitate," said Sol Bergstein, my father's long-time accountant and trusted confidante. "You either make up your mind now or somebody else is going to make it for you." Hunched over his desk, punching the air for emphasis, Sol was being, as usual, blunt and to the point. This time he didn't need to be. My father knew all too well that his company was in crisis—on the verge of bankruptcy, in fact—and that nothing was going to change unless he acted.

1

"So, I'm going to ask you one more time," Bergstein continued. "This guy sitting next to you..." Sol gestured towards me, an awkward, uncomfortable 39-year old man caught in the middle of something I wasn't at all sure I could handle. "Is he your son or is he your partner? He can't be both. If he's your partner, tell him to go to hell and give him nothing. If he's your son, give him the entire business and don't look back."

My father hesitated for just a moment. He'd worked hard all his life trying to make his company a success, and he'd achieved his goal: he'd taken us to the top of the mountain, making us one of the leading manufacturers of woman's undergarments in the world... only to watch everything start to slide downhill in recent years. He was understandably reluctant to let go, to leave behind everything he knew and enter a new phase of his life. But he was a loving man who had spent the last fifteen years sharing all his knowledge of the business with me, carefully grooming me to one day take the reins. And he also was a pragmatist; he knew when reality was staring him straight in the face.

"He's my son," Irving Tolkin finally replied as he took off his glasses and mopped his brow. "I'm going to give him the company and hope to God that he can make it work."

At that moment—a defining moment in my life—I came to two realizations. One was the recognition that my father was in essence giving me everything he owned... even though all he owned at the time was a business that was on the brink of disaster. But he was also giving me a shot at the brass ring, and if I failed, not only would I fail for myself but I'd fail for him. Now was the time for me to find out whether I could be a successful businessman or not.

In that same instant, I realized that I never wanted to face what my father had just faced. I knew that I had to do whatever was necessary to keep from ever being put in that position myself, and, more importantly, to keep my own sons from ever having to take on such an overwhelming responsibility.

That was the moment when I first started thinking about planning for the rest of my life. Until that day, I had lived like most people in their twenties and thirties, giving little consideration to the idea of saving money. The idea of preparing for my future, preparing for a time when my kids would be grown and I would be in my mid-sixties, as my father then was, had been alien to me. But in that one moment, it became a necessity.

My life would never again be the same.

SOME REALITIES ABOUT RETIREMENT

Too many people think of the day you retire as the day you start dying.

That's as wrong as wrong can be: it's actually the day you start *living*. It's the day you finally get to stop having to please others and pursue your own dreams. It's the day that making yourself happy takes top priority. Retirement isn't a release from slavery. It's a rebirth to independence.

Actually, I don't even like the *word* "retirement" because "retiring" is misleading; it implies that you're walking away from something. You're not; you're embarking on a new voyage, or at least changing the direction of the voyage... but always maintaining the momentum of the voyage, not stopping it. And the direction is actually not nearly as important as the movement.

Many of you have undoubtedly seen the television ads that feature actor Dennis Hopper addressing middle-aged viewers in hopes of getting them to patronize one particular investment company. In one of those ads, he offers the dictionary definition of the word "retirement" ("to withdraw, to go away, to disappear") but then argues that it should instead be viewed as a time to redefine. Hopper, best known for his anti-establishment roles, goes on to observe that "your generation is definitely not headed for bingo night... I just don't see you playing shuffleboard—you know what I mean?"

It's an advertisement that is not only clever and amusing, but very much on the mark. Your post-work years *should* be viewed as a time to blossom, a fresh start, not a time to withdraw and face your mortality. And there is no question that retirement today is very different than it was for our parents, or our parent's parents. As author Lee Eisenberg so eloquently describes in his excellent book *The Number*:

> "Once upon a time, the drill was to hit 65 and retire. Not long afterward, [you] kicked the bucket. People owned their homes outright, paid for things in cash. Retirement was underwritten by good old-fashioned company pensions and Social Security. The checks were as good as gold. Nobody was expected to know how to manage an elegantly diversified portfolio. The Old Rest of Your Life was about others taking some responsibility for you—your children, your ex-employer, the government."

But things are very different today. So different, in fact, that the next generation of retirees—the so-called "baby boomers" (that is, anyone born between 1946 and 1964)—will have to reinvent the entire concept from the ground up. There is, in fact, a whole new paradigm—a New Rest Of Your Life—and there are a whole slew of reasons why, as Hopper puts it, "this ain't your parents retirement." These reasons include:

- *Increased longevity due to medical advancements.* The good news is that you'll probably be able to enjoy your retirement for many, many years. Unfortunately, for many people, that's the bad news too, because spending more years on this planet without working means that you'll need a bigger nest egg to live off.

- *Increased numbers of retirees.* There will soon be more—and I mean a *lot* more—people of retirement age in the United States than ever before. Veterans returning from World War II started families in record numbers, resulting in a spike in population never seen before, or since. The first of the 78 million children they created (the baby boomer generation) have just reached retirement age, to be joined by the rest over the next two decades, thus totally swamping Social Security and Medicare systems that were created to deal with much smaller numbers.

- *Lack of preparedness, on the part of both individuals and the government.* Baby boomers, indulged by their parents, were brought up to believe in the American Dream. That's all well and good, but what they *don't* believe in is saving for a rainy day... though they do believe in living off credit, something that wasn't even an option for previous generations. The federal government has demonstrated the same remarkable faith in deficit spending yet at the same time has been lax in either foreseeing the difficulties that lie ahead or making the tough decisions necessary to repair the system.

- *Corporate greed.* Unscrupulous accounting practices in the private sector have depleted and in some cases even bankrupted many employer-sponsored pension plans. Worse yet, they have virtually eliminated pensions as a reliable source of financial support for loyal workers who have given their companies years of faithful service.

- *Fewer children to help support retirees.* Once upon a time, Ma and Pa raised a truckload of kids to help out on the farm and take over the plowing when their kinfolk reached the rocking-chair stage. Those days are long gone. In America, as in almost every developed country in the world, people are having fewer children than ever before. Smaller families means fewer people for you to turn to for help when your Social Security check just isn't enough to cover expenses, your savings have run out, and your company IRA has tanked.

Those of you who are interested in a deeper understanding of these underlying factors should turn to the Appendix in the back of this book. You may learn some very surprising facts about retirement and the way it's evolved through the years... as well as the way it's likely to change in the years ahead.

The bottom line is this: One day you will stop working, whether voluntarily or involuntarily. And when that day comes, a lot of questions will rear their ugly heads, questions like: How can you possibly survive without that steady paycheck? Who will watch over you? Will your pension still be in existence when you need it? Will government entitlements like Social Security be able to support you? Sadly, the answer to the latter two questions is probably no. For numerous reasons (which are elaborated on in the aforementioned Appendix), you can't count on Social

Security—at least not in its present form—any more than you can count on that dicey pension plan your company may have offered.

I have a friend—a very wealthy, very lucky friend—who has twenty million dollars. He put it all in tax-free bonds, and he gets 5 percent interest—a million dollars a year—and he lives on that million dollars every year without having to pay any taxes. That's great... but how many people can accumulate twenty million dollars in liquid assets? For the rest of us, we have to find another way, because we don't have that luxury.

At the other end of the continuum, I knew a woman who worked in a hospital for 34 years. She was still working at the age of 66, when she unfortunately fell down a flight of stairs and died as a result of her injuries. This was someone who always cut corners. She'd brown-bag her lunches, wear the same clothes for years on end, deny herself the finer things in life. As a result, at the time of her death she had accumulated $600,000, which she left to her two children... who proceeded to take the $300,000 each, and in one year, blew it all. This woman lived her entire life so that her two kids could have one year of extravagance. What a tragedy.

PLANNING IS EVERYTHING

Author John M. Richardson, Jr. once observed, "When it comes to the future, there are three kinds of people: those who let it happen, those who make it happen, and those who wonder what happened." If you don't want to be one of those people who spend the rest of their lives wondering what might have been, you have to plan ahead. In fact, I'll take it a step further: *planning for your retirement is as necessary as breathing.*

The cold, hard fact is that most people will find it very difficult to maintain anything close to their current lifestyle in

7

their postretirement years unless they have done a good deal of planning in their *pre*retirement years. That said, you can't just plan randomly, with some vague goal in mind. You have to be smart, and you have to ask the right questions. You have to know what it is you want to do in the last third of your life and then you have to take the actions that allow you to accomplish your goals.

Unfortunately, almost nobody is doing it. As Lee Eisenberg puts it,

> "[Most baby boomers] never get around to learning how money works, how it grows, how others make money off it, how it can be spread around various types of assets to optimize returns and minimize risk. They have other things on their minds. They get out of college and start working—if they're lucky enough to land a job—then decide they've made the wrong career choice and spend a few years retooling their qualifications. Then big changes kick in. Marriage. Domestic partnership. Civil union. He works. She works. Kids wander into the picture. Nobody has any time. No time to plan. No time to save. A little time to shop. It's hard. It's complicated."

It may be hard to find the time to plan for your future, but as we'll see shortly, it's not necessarily complicated. Nonetheless, Eisenberg's words translate into concrete figures. Less than a quarter of today's workers over the age of fifty have saved $100,000 or more, and the net worth of today's average baby boomer is just a meager $25,000.

How can you possibly live off of a life savings of $25,000? You can't. Yet many baby boomers are living from paycheck to paycheck. They have no savings and no investments, and little or no tangible net worth. I know lots of people who led very good lives while they were working, but they have nothing now. Don't do any planning and don't take any risks and you'll likely end up right in that average, or worse: with less than $25,000 in assets and 30+ years of your life left to live.

If you're the kind of person who likes to live for the day and be spontaneous, consider this: if you don't plan for something important, there are often unpleasant repercussions. Your boss may pass over you for a promotion because you didn't get your business presentation together in time to rehearse it sufficiently and impress a potential client. That party you want to throw may be a bust due to insufficient food, insufficient drink, or poor attendance (maybe you mailed the invitations out too late). Your relationship with your children may fracture because you consistently fail to set aside time to attend school functions or sporting events.

Simply put, you can't *not* plan without unintended consequences following in the wake. You simply cannot expect that things will somehow take care of themselves; sticking your head in the sand may be feasible if you happen to be an ostrich, but it's not an option for anyone who wants to have a fulfilling retirement. Doing so relinquishes control of your own fate, and that in turn will affect everybody around you. Everyone you are close to and everyone you love will suffer along with you, so if you don't do this kind of planning for yourself, do it for them. Lack of planning can affect everyone you have a relationship with, everyone you're responsible for, everyone you might be able to help... or anyone you might have to someday turn to *for* help. You lose all the way down the line if you don't plan.

Hopefully these words will serve as a wake-up call. And the sooner you start this planning, the better off you'll be. True, it's best done in your thirties or forties because that will give your assets a chance to appreciate substantially, but it's never too late to start. The good news is that even if you start as late as today, you can still do lots of positive things for your future... as long as you're willing to take action. And don't worry—once you get past any irrational fears you may have of preparing for your retirement, the planning will take on a momentum of its own and can even be fun, especially if you follow your passion.

SURVIVING RETIREMENT FINANCIALLY

With the future of both government entitlements and company pensions iffy at best, baby boomers are going to have to take financial responsibility for their own retirement. Add in factors like rising longevity, soaring health-care costs, and falling asset returns, and it's clear that today's workers will have to save significantly more than their parents did.

If you think about it logically, there are really only two ways to be able to survive retirement financially:

1. Plan ahead so that you have sufficient funds to maintain your present standard of living for the rest of your life— and you really should figure on living to 90 or beyond. This requires a substantial amount of principal so that the interest alone can support you at that level, because invading the principal lowers the amount of interest that gets paid out. You may need to work more years to accumulate these funds, though it can sometimes be difficult to find a new job after the age of 50. (Workers in physically demanding

jobs have an especially tough time extending their careers.)

2. Lower your expectations and plan on cutting back after you retire. Most people can trim their expenses by at least a certain percentage without it significantly altering their lifestyle.

Personally, I'm of the belief that you shouldn't be forced to cut back, not even one percent. By focusing on planning instead of cutting corners, you can have more than enough assets to not only live your preretirement lifestyle but a dramatically *improved* lifestyle.

Traditional financial planners recommend that people approaching retirement age take the following steps:

1. Pay down your debt, especially high interest credit cards.

2. Step up your savings. Ideally they should be 10 to 20 percent of your annual income, and you should put as much as possible into tax-deferred accounts like IRAs and 401(k) plans.

3. Diversify your investments.

4. Solidify your health and life insurance policies. Take a long-term care policy if you can afford it—something that's especially important because it allows you to protect your assets while providing for treatment and therapies that Medicare or private health insurance won't pay for.

5. Work longer, even part-time.

This is all basically good advice, though there's really much more you can do to help yourself, as you'll learn in these pages. I'm an especially big advocate of working beyond the time you formally retire; in fact, as you'll see in Chapter Ten, I advise people to work for as long as they are physically and mentally able—right up until the day you die if you can do so. The benefits to continuing to work and be a productive member of society go far beyond financial ones, although the monetary incentives alone are huge: if you're willing to work even an extra few years beyond the minimum retirement age of 62, you can increase your retirement income tremendously. Why such a huge payoff? There are several reasons:

1. Because you earn more income, you can save more.

2. Because you won't have to invade your IRA or other savings, it, along with all your other existing assets, will continue to grow.

3. By paying into the system longer, you increase your lifetime Social Security benefits.

4. Your annual Social Security benefits also increase, since the lifetime benefits are withdrawn over a shorter period of time.

The Dark Cloud... And The Silver Lining

There are many compelling reasons to face your retirement years with a sense of optimism, and we'll explore all of them in great detail, but you also need to accept some harsh reality. The inescapable fact is that the baby boom generation is now on the cusp of retirement, with the oldest boomers just about to hit that magic age that Paul McCartney sang about. As this huge generation makes its way out of the labor force, it will have to do so on much different terms than those offered workers during the late 20th century.

So you need to understand that whatever you had during your working life, you're not going to be able to continue that lifestyle unless you take steps to help yourself. Whatever your age, you'd better start the planning process *now* because the government is not going to be there for you, and, in all probability, neither will your employer. Social Security is in trouble, Medicare is in trouble, and the organizations that were developed to provide support services for retirees—the non-profit organizations that run the senior citizen centers and provide other vital services—are going to be overwhelmed by the increasing numbers of the senior population.

Everything's going to change in the next twenty or thirty years: demographics, the environment, our energy sources, government policy. The idea is to see *beyond* those changes. That's where opportunity lies. On the other hand, if you do not adjust for change and do not prepare for it, you're facing struggle, uncertainty, fear. That's what I say to people who feel that they simply want to maintain the status quo for the rest of their lives, that it's good enough to keep things same as they ever were. No, you'll need to do a lot better than that because you simply cannot live on hope—you have to live on reality.

If you face that reality squarely, if you're prepared to do some creative thinking and sensible planning, you can enjoy the kind of retirement you may have only thought was the stuff of dreams. I know. I'm living proof that it works.

Now let me tell you how I did it.

CHAPTER TWO

MY PLAN

"Master of my fate, captain of my soul"
—from the poem Invictus
by William Ernest Henley

Back in the very first year of our marriage, when she was just 20 and I was 22, my wife Estelle and I had a long discussion about money. We had seen various family members—aunts, uncles, cousins—struggling financially, and we saw the toll that stress placed on their lives. There and then we made the decision that we would never ask anyone for money, ever. She would do what she had to do, and I would do what I had to do, to make sure that never happened. We never wanted to turn to our parents or our friends, and most of all, we never wanted to turn to our children. We determined that we would always be self-sufficient.

At the time, we didn't have the resources to do anything about it. Eventually that changed, though. After years of struggle and sacrifice, I was able to not only return my father's company to significant profitability but expand its horizons tremendously. Slowly but surely, I began developing the financial means to create a fulfilling, happy, and rewarding retirement for Estelle and me.

Even after I had sufficient finances, the question was, how to best accomplish that? I had already come to realize that the stock market wasn't for me. From my perspective, it was simply the legal equivalent to a roulette wheel... and I wasn't prepared to put my hard-earned money on seven red. I decided instead that I wanted to invest in things that either appreciated or created income. To me, that seemed the most logical way for us to be able to maintain our lifestyle—or perhaps even improve it— after I was no longer bringing in a paycheck.

But what should I invest in? That was the problem I wrestled with for a long time. One day, out of the blue, the solution came to me. And it was simplicity itself: *Marry time to money.* In other words, I would invest only in things that would occupy me productively—hobbies I enjoyed, interests I had, objects that I loved, businesses that I was familiar with. This way, I would end up owning assets that would, with luck, not only gain value monetarily but would also give me a new focus, a source of stimulation outside of my work life. Just as importantly, I decided to invest only in things I understood well and could therefore exert some degree of control over.

As you will see, the financial strategy I evolved over time was anything but conventional. It will also become obvious that not everything I invested in worked out... although those that did more than made up for the failures. Yet I feel that even the failures worked to my advantage because each added to my body of knowledge—I learned what *not* to do as well as what to do— therefore improving the odds of each subsequent investment. Mistakes, I came to realize, were in fact crucial to the process... as long as you learned from them and adjusted accordingly.

They say that hindsight is 20/20. Now that I'm able to look back on things, I can see that my plan included the following key elements, even though many of them weren't apparent to me at the time:

- The concept of marrying time to money.
- Diversity.
- An element of risk...which increased the chances of success.
- An emphasis on quality.
- Help from experts.
- A definitive exit strategy for each component.

Here is a detailed description of the various investments I made for my future, presented in chronological order.

STAMP BUSINESS

The first aspect of my retirement plan started out not as a money-making enterprise, but simply as a way to bond with my son Larry.

At an early age, Larry had developed an affinity for collecting stamps—something that delighted me since it had been a childhood hobby of mine too. Actually, I discovered his interest in philately almost by accident. In 1959, I was on a business trip in Rome when, on a whim, I decided to visit the Vatican post office and buy a fairly complete collection of all their stamps—I literally said to the clerk, "Give me one of everything." It cost me maybe thirty or forty dollars, and when I got home I put the stamps away and forgot about them.

A few years later, Larry surprised me by announcing that he had taken those stamps to Gimbel's—one of the big retailers in New York that had a stamp department—and that they had told him that the stamps were now worth eighty dollars. It didn't make sense to me. I assumed Larry had it wrong—after all,

17

he was just twelve years old at the time. So the next day I took the stamps myself to Gimbel's and the clerk confirmed that that was indeed what they were worth. In a relatively short space of time, my money had more than doubled.

That gave me an idea. I began to think that collecting stamps would be a wonderful thing for me to do when I retired, because it was something I had always loved... plus it was something special I could share with my son. I began thinking that this could be a source of both pleasure and profitability, and, perhaps most importantly, it would consume my time when I was no longer working. Soon we swung into full gear and began attending stamp auctions and sales. We weren't making big money—a few hundred here, a few hundred there—but the business was good enough, and it was enjoyable.

A couple of years later I began thinking that it made sense to focus on investing in stamps from those countries that were most likely to grow economically in the years ahead. One of the countries I picked was Japan. That turned out to be one of my best investments—don't forget, this was back in the 1960s, when Japan was just about to explode economically, kind of like China is today. We bought full dealer stocks of Japanese stamps—a hundred copies of almost every stamp—and, to our delight, the demand for them began going through the roof.

Eventually, though, prices began to plateau, making it obvious that the stamp market had peaked, and so we began to wind things down. But it turned out to be a really good investment nonetheless. In fact, just a few years ago, I opted to liquidate most of my remaining stamps so Larry and I took a booth at one of the big shows and we set a 40 or 50 percent mark-up on all the stamps we wanted to sell. The attendees were dealers—not consumers—but even though they were used to paying rock-bottom wholesale prices, they came by the booth in droves and were almost fighting to buy our stamps!

The real value of this first phase of my retirement plan was not monetary, however. It was that it showed me how important it was to *marry time to money*. From then on, it became just as important to me to find investments that would utilize my time productively as it was to find those that would be profitable. The emphasis had shifted subtly: My goal now was to identify those things that would keep me busy, keep me interested, follow my passion, and give me purpose... as well as make money.

A Postscript: Online selling through companies like eBay has totally changed the world of buying and selling, and not taking advantage of it is, in my opinion, tantamount to financial suicide. Today the market is wide open: the owner of an item can sell directly to someone who wants to own it, eliminating all the people in the middle (the dealers who take the bulk of the profit). A case in point: Several years ago, a dealer offered me $800 for part of my Japanese stamp collection. I declined, and a short time later Larry listed the same exact stamps on eBay. Over time, selling them piecemeal, we made many thousands of dollars instead.

Lessons learned: Only invest in quality... and be aware of changes in the market. The more quality you have, the longer it retains its value, and the more you stay current with market fluctuations, the better you're going to do in the long run.

MICHIGAN APPAREL STORES

About five years after my company started becoming successful, I met a buyer by the name of Jayne. Jayne worked for the company

19

that owned the biggest retail store in Kalamazoo, Michigan. She was pleasant and knowledgeable, but she was very unhappy with the way things were going at work. One day she came to me and said, "You know, Marvin, I'd really like to go out on my own." I said, "Do it; you're a very capable woman." The problem was that she didn't have enough money to start up a business of her own, so I offered to put up $15,000 to match the $15,000 she had saved up, and we went into business together. We decided that my role would be to do the bookkeeping—something I had gotten quite good at in my own business—and her role would be to do the buying and run the stores.

The first store we opened up was in Muskegon, Michigan. Within a year, the store was doing well enough that we were both able to take out our initial $15,000 investment; from that point on, everything the store earned was going to be gravy. Things were rolling along nicely, and we soon opened a second store in a shopping center in Kalamazoo, then a third store in a place called Grand Haven, and then a fourth one in Grand Rapids.

We wound up with seven stores. Jayne did extremely well when she only had one store to look after, and she still was able to stay on top of things when there were two or three of them, but by the time she got to the seventh store she was overwhelmed.

It soon became apparent that we were losing money. Finally, I felt I had to cut my losses, but I also wanted to be fair to Jayne. I told her, "Among all the stores, we now only have $75,000 worth of assets. Look, I'm doing well in my own business, so I don't want the money. You take the $75,000 and we'll close the stores, and call it a day."

But Jayne said no. She was sure that she could turn things around, but sadly, my instincts were correct. After a few months of struggle, we ended up having to close all the stores, and Jayne lost the $75,000 she could have taken out of the business. But we've remained friends and she's made wise investments with the money she made since, so she's doing all right.

That was an aspect of my retirement planning that didn't work out as I had hoped. I had thought that helping to run the stores would keep me busy and make me some money, but it wasn't to be. There were a myriad of reasons why the business failed: the high cost of rent, customer pilferage, and difficulty controlling inventory and personnel because the multiple stores were spread over too wide a geographic area—it was simply too difficult logistically for Jayne to oversee everything. We also fell into the trap of expanding too quickly—a common cause of business failure. Mind you, I didn't lose money on the deal, but the idea just didn't work out as we'd hoped it would.

Lessons learned: This was a good venture with definite potential. But one person who's successful in one venture may not have the same success in several ventures. You simply can't have your butt in seven different places at once.

Another important lesson I learned from this experience is, when things turn sour for whatever reason, cut your losses. All the people involved in this venture were smart, honest, and hard-working, but it had nothing to do with that. Things happened that were simply out of their control; they were overwhelmed by circumstance.

SWIMSUIT COMPANY

This was a venture I went into with a close personal friend named Les. Les had two kids who were the same age as my oldest two sons—a boy and a girl, both of whom were grade-A swimmers.

21

One day he came to me and said he thought he could design a racing swimsuit that was better than anything that was out there. Speedo was already the big name in swimwear, but they only made nylon swimsuits at the time, and nylon wasn't as suitable as some newer fabrics that had been introduced at the time.

Les had a good idea but no capital, so I went to a large manufacturer that I had a business relationship with. They made one of those newer fabrics that had fabulous stretching qualities, so I felt they might be willing to partner with us. As it turned out, they wanted to have a big presence in the swimsuit business, and I convinced them that we were onto something, so they gave us $25,000 in startup money and we set up a company called AquaFree. As I had done with Jayne, my job was to look after the books; Les's job was to do the designing.

He based his concept on the fact that trapped water increases a swimmer's weight and thus inhibits their ability to swim fast. With a conventional woman's swimsuit, the water goes in around the breast area and is trapped inside because of the tight elastic around the arms and legs. Les's idea—for which he received a patent— was that if he used a mesh instead of a solid piece in the front of the suit, the water would be able to leave and therefore allow the swimmer to swim faster. He also designed men's swimsuits with mesh on the side, allowing water build-up to escape.

Because his kids were involved in organized swimming events, Les knew all the coaches at many different high schools and colleges, and so we started to sell our suits very, very well. We were delivering two thousand dollars worth of product every week. I thought we had a big business; it seemed like everything was going along fine.

And it was... except what we didn't factor in was that competitive swimmers spend about six to eight hours in chlorinated water every single day. And, to our dismay, we soon discovered that the fabric we were using was not completely impervious to the chemicals that keep swimming pools clean. What would happen—especially with the girl's suits, which had the center mesh—was that the swimmers wound up nearly naked because the fabric deteriorated and became transparent.

The returns started coming in, along with perfectly justifiable complaints from upset customers. Les and I knew we had to find a fabric that was resistant to chlorine, so we went to a different manufacturer. Their version of the fabric, through some special treatment, was capable of withstanding the chlorine. But by that time our reputation was shot—nobody would buy from us because they didn't trust us. We sold off our remaining stock cheap, and that was the end of AquaFree.

Obviously, this was one investment that did not work out, but it was a very interesting experiment... and it was fun. Plus, we didn't have to put up any money of our own, so all we lost was our time. Les and I still remain friends; he didn't do anything wrong, it's just that neither of us knew that the swimsuit fabric dissolved in chlorine!

In retrospect, I can see that we could have remanufactured the suits with the second manufacturer's fabric and marketed them under a different name, but I got busy with other things and I decided that I needed the aggravation like a hole in the head. So I cut my losses and walked away.

Lessons learned: Have more patience. This was something that didn't work out but could have been extremely successful if I'd just done more research and tested my product more thoroughly before marketing it. I also should have been willing to adapt and move in a different direction when things started falling apart (literally), but I was so wrapped up in other aspects of my life that I couldn't devote the time or energy to make it work. Basically, like Jayne, I had my butt on too many chairs. And when you do that—if you'll pardon the pun—something's bound to fall through the cracks.

BUYING FABERGE

One rainy autumn morning, Estelle and I were walking around Paris, dodging the raindrops. I was on a business trip and I was tired and really didn't want to go shopping, but we came across a store that was selling Russian artifacts, and their window display caught our eye, so we went inside. My grandparents had come over from Russia, and as I began looking around, I started thinking that it would be fitting if my retirement strategy had some relationship with my heritage.

The shopkeeper was an elderly man, and there was nobody else in the store so he started to chat with us. He began by telling us, "I knew Carl Faberge." I learned from him that Carl Faberge had been the goldsmith and jeweller to the Russian Imperial Court but after the revolution had fled to Switzerland, where he died in 1920. The shopkeeper told me that if I was seeking objects that would appreciate in value, this was something I should invest in, because Faberge made a practice of destroying all his irregulars. As a result, every Faberge item on the market was perfect.

For the next six hours, this kindly old man proceeded to give Estelle and me a thorough lesson in everything Faberge, and the essence of his lesson was: Always buy the most expensive item you can afford. If your budget is five hundred dollars, buy a single high-quality five hundred dollar item; if you can stretch to a thousand, buy a one thousand dollar item. I only bought one Faberge object that day: a small spoon with a "Chai" (the

Hebrew word for "life") inscribed on it. It spoke to me; it said, "Buy me," so I did. It cost me $900 and I still own it... and you can't buy it from me because it still talks to me.

The old man had sparked a passion in me for buying Faberge and so, on my next trip to Paris, I revisited the shop but it still just had mostly the same items I had seen before. I asked the shopkeeper to tell me where else I could go to see more Faberge objects, and he referred me to a store in London called Wartski.

On my next trip to London I went there and the manager, a very nice young man by the name of Geoff, began showing me his inventory. Everything was gorgeous, but very expensive—three thousand dollars and up for a single piece. But I remembered what the old man had told me, and my business was starting to do really well at that time, so I decided to buy three or four pieces. They were worth about $25,000 in total, but not only did I not have that kind of money with me, I knew it would take some time to put it together. I told Geoff, "I want these pieces, but it will probably take me a year to pay you."

To my utter surprise, he said, "Take them."

I was amazed. I asked, "Don't you want some collateral from me?"

He said, "No, take them. I trust you." To this day, I haven't the slightest idea why he trusted me so much after just one visit, but of course I paid the bill over the next few months and eventually Geoff and I became great friends.

I went back to the Paris store a couple more times after that, but the old shopkeeper had died and his son didn't have any real enthusiasm for the business, so from that point on Geoff became my adviser in all things Faberge. He steered me towards every piece I bought thereafter, and he made sure that everything I picked out was the cream of the crop.

Over the next twenty years I acquired more than thirty Faberge pieces. They weren't the famous Faberge eggs because those were out of my price range, but, thanks to Geoff, everything I did buy was top quality. Eventually, though, I decided to sell most of my Faberge pieces. Beyond the fact that I suspected they had appreciated substantially, I realized that I couldn't leave them to my family, because how would you divide them up? I was secure in the knowledge that I would get true value for them because I was dealing with people I knew and could trust.

I was right. When I finally brought them to Christies for evaluation many years later, their expert was practically drooling. Most of my pieces sold at auction for many times what I had paid for them; in fact, the London store bought back a number of them at a premium, giving me a substantial profit.

My experience with collecting Faberge was as good as it gets. Not only was it one of the best-performing investments I had, it occupied my time productively—I kept going to auctions, kept investing, and Geoff made sure that I only bought the best. In every aspect, it was totally fulfilling. Not only was it interesting to learn about Faberge and his art, it was wonderful to own these little objects that I loved so much.

A Postscript: The post-cold war economy has made a lot of Russians rich. Flush with oil money, many of them are investing in their heritage, and as a result, the value of Faberge pieces has skyrocketed in the last few years. With the benefit of hindsight, I realize that I made a mistake by selling mine when I did; had I waited just a little longer and been a little better at reading the economic climate, my profits would have been substantially larger.

Lessons learned: As the old man in Paris taught me, always buy the most expensive item you can afford. But by virtue of his knowledge and integrity—and that of Geoff—another important lesson I learned is to do business only with the top people in the field. Go to the experts who recognize quality, who know what they're doing, and who know what the market is. And when circumstances dictate that you consider parting with tangible items, always try to look forward and not back. Timing can be everything!

BUYING ART

Some people invest in Van Goghs or Picassos, but that's out of my league, so I knew that if I wanted to get into art I would have to do things in a more modest way. I decided that here, as in all the other aspects of my retirement planning, the best approach was to follow my passion, so I simply bought things that I liked. That gave me not only enjoyment of the items, but investment potential as well.

Some thirty years ago I bought four Irving Penn photographs. They were part of a numbered, limited edition and they cost me $3,000 apiece. Not long ago I saw that an auction house was going to be selling some photographs, so out of curiousity I looked in the catalog and they had one of the Irving Penns that I owned... and it was presold. I called and was told it had sold for $48,000. Sure, it took twenty years to reach that value, but that's still a 1600% appreciation—not too shabby.

I started buying collectible dishes too, and there's an interesting story about how I got into it. Way back in 1959, Estelle and I were in Denmark. We were strolling down the street one day when a Royal Copenhagen store caught our eye. Estelle liked one particular set of dishes called Flora Danica. We decided to get a service for eight, with a few extra pieces, and the bill came to $400, which I thought was very reasonable for such good quality china. As I was writing the check, I asked the salesman casually when we could expect delivery. He said he'd have to ask his manager. When he returned, his response staggered me.

Seven years!

When I picked myself up from the floor, I said, "You're telling me I'm going to have to wait seven *years* for these dishes? I may not even live that long!" It was ridiculous to me—how could they expect a customer to wait seven years?? He explained that the dishes were all hand-painted and that's how long it would take for them to be produced. But I thought it was nuts, and I said to Estelle, "Please, honey, pick out a set we can get right away—I'm not waiting seven years for a set of dishes." So she did—a very nice Wild Rose set, also made by Royal Copenhagen.

Some twenty years later, I found myself in a fine china shop in London; we had bought some pottery from them previously and I knew the salesmen there. While browsing, I spotted a plate with the exact same Flora Danica pattern Estelle and I had seen back in 1959, and I idly asked the clerk what the price was.

"A thousand U.S. dollars," he told me.

I looked at him warily. "You mean a thousand dollars for the set, don't you?"

"No, sir. Just that one plate."

Again I was speechless. When I could get my mouth working once more I told the salesman I'd had an opportunity to buy an entire service for eight with that same exact pattern for $400. He said, "Sure, but that would have been twenty years ago"... and he was right! I was flabbergasted... and I was furious with myself for having not placed that order.

I vowed then and there never to make that kind of mistake

again. Over the next few years, I bought not one but two Flora Danica sets, piecemeal, and I got a lot of pleasure out of owning and looking at them—pleasure that was further enhanced by knowing how much they were appreciating monetarily.

It's important to understand that I bought all these things primarily because I liked them. Sure, the investment potential factored in. But even if an expert had advised me that the items I was interested in were overpriced, I probably would have bought them anyway. After all, if you really like something and you know you're going to enjoy having it, overpaying for it is not a big deal. Yes, it may in essence mean losing money, but only at the point of purchase; you have no way of knowing what the value will be years down the road, so you may end up making money on the item even if you initially overpaid.

This aspect of my retirement plan also helped me discover something about myself: it gave me confirmation that I have good taste. Psychologically, it's very uplifting if you invest in a multitude of artifacts and see most, if not all of them, appreciate in value. You say to yourself, gee, I must have good aesthetic sensibilities—I picked this picture or that object, and I bought it just because I loved it, whether it cost a hundred dollars or a thousand dollars. That makes you feel good, and it doesn't have to happen with everything you buy, either. You can't expect to go to the horse races and pick the winning horse in every race: nobody's good enough to do that. You'll certainly pick some losers too... but as long as most of your selections are winners, you'll walk away happy.

Lessons learned: Follow your passion and trust your instincts. If an item "speaks" to you and you know instinctively that you will enjoy looking at it through the years, that's reason enough to own it.

That said, try to buy quality items from recognized artists wherever possible. And check the market frequently to see how well your collectibles are appreciating! Again, timing can be everything.

SWEATER COMPANY

At one point, I employed a talented salesman out on the West Coast by the name of Steve. He eventually left my company and went to work for a sportswear outfit in Los Angeles, where he became very successful selling sweaters at the wholesale level. After a few years of doing that, Steve came to me and told me that he wanted to go into business for himself, and he asked me if I knew anyone who manufactured sweaters.

Through my business contacts, I knew a young man based in Taiwan named George. I put Steve in touch with George to see if he could make the garments Steve wanted, or if he knew someone who could make them. George came back to me and said, "Marvin, I can do this, and I can do it at the right price." I thought that was great, so I asked Steve how much money he needed to get the business off the ground, and he told me that he needed $70,000 as startup money. I then asked him for projections and he told me that within six months he expected to generate $6 million in sales.

It sounded good to me, so I put up the money. Over the next few months George made the samples and Steve left the company he had been working for in LA... but of course he still retained his contacts with the buyers at all the stores throughout the country because he had been selling them hundreds of millions of dollars worth of sportswear each year.

At the end of the first three months, Steve had sold about $2 million worth of sweaters, but over the next three months they only went up to $3.5 million. I reminded him that he had told me he could do $6 million in business in the first six months, and he asked for another two or three months to make that goal. Somewhat reluctantly, I agreed, but even with the extra time he never was able to boost sales above that $3.5 million mark.

At that point, I said, "Steve, you didn't do what you said you were going to do." I had learned a long time ago that the first losses are the cheapest losses. I could see clearly that I wasn't going to get my $70,000 back, so I made the decision to simply kiss it goodbye and write it off. (One of the many wonderful things about the capitalist system in this country is that the government is a partner in your losses as well as in your profits.) Sometimes it's just easier to walk away and admit to yourself that your money is gone than to hang on and hope things will turn around; putting good money after bad usually only adds to the problem. So I told Steve, "You do it with George; you guys are on your own."

For a while I lost touch with both men, but then a few years later George called and told me that he had invested another $250,000 but was planning to sue to get his money back. I advised George to do the same as I had done— I felt he should simply accept that he was never going to get his money back and he should just walk away. I have reason to believe he eventually did sue Steve regardless, but I don't think he actually collected anything.

This was another reflection of my desire to invest in something that I thought had potential, in an area where I had some knowledge. The mistake I made was that I invested in someone who wasn't competent, or wasn't honest, or some combination of the two. Analyze it any way you want; it was simply a bad situation. George lost his money, I lost my money, and that was that. It was an idea that simply didn't work.

Lessons learned: Too many excuses and too little professionalism spells trouble. When somebody makes a promise and doesn't keep it, walk away. Quickly.

BUYING GOLD AND COLLECTIBLE COINS

By this point, my retirement plan was in full swing. Despite the fact that I had already made some mistakes and suffered some losses (which is all part of the game: see Chapter Six), I was still searching for investments that would both appreciate and occupy my time productively in my post-work years. So, in the interest of diversification, I decided to supplement my stamp investment with gold coins.

In 1982, my company opened a manufacturing plant in China. A few months later, I was discussing investments with a friend named Milt. It turned out that we both had an interest in buying gold, and that got me thinking that we should actively pursue it. I had another friend by the name of Louis who ran a big coin store (which eventually became such a success that it turned into a bank) so Milt and I went to see him, with the idea of buying some Krugerrands (South African coins), each of which contained one ounce of gold. Louis informed us that the Chinese government had just come out with a Panda coin which also contained an ounce of gold, and since it was the first time the Chinese government had issued a gold coin in many, many years, he advised us to buy those instead.

I could immediately sense a synergy: I'd opened up my Chinese plant the same year their government issued the Panda coin. It just felt right to buy it, plus an expert was recommending it. So Milt and I each bought twenty-five of them, paying about three hundred dollars apiece. I put my $7,500 worth of gold coins in the bank vault and forgot about them.

About eight years later, Milt phoned and said that he'd just read in a coin magazine that the Panda was now selling for a thousand dollars, even though gold itself hadn't gone up substantially. I called Louis and asked him why the price had shot up so high. He said he didn't have the slightest idea, but advised us to hang on to the coins because he had a sense that they might go up further still.

Now my interest was piqued. I got a subscription to the leading coin magazine so that I could keep an eye on the price. In February, they announced that the Panda had gone up to $1,400; by March, it was $1,800; in April it was $2,300; in May, $2,700; in June, $3,200; in July, $3,600. In August, it hit $4,000 a coin. I now owned $100,000 worth of Pandas!

I called Milt and said, "I think we've got the only fifty coins left; that's the only logical explanation as to why the price is so high." I felt if we sold off all our coins it would flood the market and force the price down, so we had to be careful. I started looking for ads taken by people who wanted to buy Pandas. I found two collectors willing to pay $4,000 per coin and we sold them five coins each. Then I called Louis and offered him some coins at a slight discount—after all, he was the guy who recommended them to us in the first place. So we each sold him five more coins for $3,800 each... at which point Milt went out and bought a Cadillac and a house in the country.

Eight months later, the same Pandas were selling for $800 a coin. But we did fine—we sold thirty out of the fifty we had and got our money out of the investment when it was sky-high. I still have my ten remaining Pandas. And to this day, I can't tell you why they went up to $4,000, or why they went back down to $800.

Lessons learned: Have patience. Not everything turns over quickly. Over years, something like gold will usually appreciate, but you have to have patience with it. The good thing about gold is that you can take your profit and then go right back into the market—sell it high, then buy it back low just days or weeks later. It's not like buying foodstuffs that can go stale: gold is forever.

FLORIDA DRUGSTORE CHAIN

This was one investment which proved that I'm not always right.

Back in the mid-1970s, the aging population in Florida was starting to grow dramatically. One of my dearest friends told me that he and his stockbroker had decided to invest in a chain of drug stores down there. They invited me to join them, and I thought to myself, how can this lose?

I put in about $30,000. I had the resources at the time and I thought it was a real winner, so I did it, and that's how I became one of the original owners of a chain of drugstores in Florida.

I even checked in on my investment from time to time. It so happened that one of the stores was located just a block away from where my mother lived in Hollywood, Florida, so every time I visited her I made a point of stopping in. The store was always busy as hell. There were all these high-rises all around, filled with elderly people buying prescription drugs and over-the-counter items as fast as they could be put on the shelves.

The chain stayed in business for fifteen years, but I never saw a cent. I couldn't prove it in a court of law, but it's my belief that those responsible mismanaged the investment along with dissipating all the profits. Suspiciously, they retired soon after the company went bankrupt and the stores were closed. I went down to Florida to talk to them, and they gave me a hundred reasons why the investment failed, but all I know is that every time I went in there, the stores were busy.

It's a shame, because if the management had been more scrupulous, I'm sure we would all have done well out of this investment. Sadly, though, greed and poor judgement can undo even the best planning.

Lessons learned: Do your homework, and always check the reputation of the people who are behind the investment. Keep close tabs on their performance, because mismanagement trumps even potential. And make sure you have a clear exit strategy so you can get out quickly and easily if things go bad.

REAL ESTATE TAX SHELTERS

Real estate. Sure thing. Can't miss. Right?
Wrong.

My business eventually became so successful that we were making substantial profits even after all the salaries and overheads were paid. But with big profits come big taxes and when I began seeing the size of the checks we were writing to the IRS I started asking my accountants how we could keep a little more of our hard-earned money and use it more productively.

There were, of course, all kinds of people calling me day and night with all kinds of investment offers at the time. All the big investment companies and all the big brokers were on the phone constantly trying to sell me one thing or another. But after a friend and I had bought and sold a commercial building in Brooklyn at a substantial profit, I started thinking about investing in real estate as a tax shelter.

A short time later, I heard about an opportunity to get in on the ground floor with a group that was investing in high-rise commercial buildings in top midtown Manhattan locations. I met with them and they explained to me that if I were to join the venture, the investment would be tax-free until or unless I cashed out. I thought, what can go wrong?

Sol Bergstein, my accountant, was completely against the idea. He told me I would be making a big mistake and he warned me that I would be in over my head with this. He advised me to instead put my profits in bonds—they were paying 16 or 17 percent interest at the time—and pay my taxes, and be happy.

But I didn't listen. The first investment I made with this group was great... which, of course, is how you get sucked in. But every further investment I made with them—and I bought shares in several buildings—was an unmitigated disaster. The reason, I was to learn later, was that the properties were over-leveraged; the group were selling shares that amounted to far more money than the building could possibly be worth in twenty years. Exacerbating things, rent rolls didn't go up the way they had predicted, and then Congress under President Reagan changed the laws regulating this kind of activity, effectively killing it as a viable investment.

But there was even worse news. It turns out that when this particular kind of investment goes bad, you suffer a double whammy: not only do you lose all the money that you put in, the IRS makes you pay taxes on those lost monies as well.

I thought this was the right way to go, but I was wrong. With 20/20 hindsight I can see that the people who organized this investment group could not be trusted. Were they running a scam, or were they simply misguided? I wouldn't bet either explanation was wrong. Certainly nothing they did was illegal. But they were the general partners, the people who put up little or no money. It was only the big investors—the limited partners like me—that got burned.

Lessons learned: If it seems too good to be true, it *is* too good to be true. I never thought that property investments—especially in a real estate market like midtown Manhattan—could possibly fail, but fail they did. As a corollary, I also learned never to invest in anything that's overly complicated or too difficult to understand. And I realized that, if you have a smart accountant, he's probably a lot smarter than you are. Even if he isn't, you need to trust his instincts. By this point in my career I was a fairly savvy businessman but in this case I was way over my head. Sol Bergstein knew even less about the details than I did, but he knew that it was a mistake, and I should have listened to him. It cost me many thousands of dollars to find that out; this had been my single biggest investment to date. If I had taken that money and put it into Faberge instead, it would have appreciated enormously instead of evaporating. But I got greedy...and I paid the price. Sometimes success makes you stupid.

THE VALUE OF MY BUSINESS

Later in this book, I'll tell you the story of how I took my father's failing children's underwear company and transformed it into a successful lingerie and sleepwear business. Once the tide had turned, it became apparent that the biggest asset I had was the value of my company, and so it became the mainstay of my retirement planning. I knew that I'd have to oversee the business with that in mind, so that it could ultimately create enough money for me to do all the other things I wanted to do with my life.

For now, suffice it to say that, through a lot of hard work and creative thinking, my partners and I were able to turn the company around and make it profitable—eventually extremely profitable. That not only allowed me to draw a good salary, but also drove the value of the company up. When I finally retired, I decided to sell my shares in the business to my children. But first, I found a clever attorney who was able to set things up so that I am, to this day, able to draw significant income from the sale of those shares. Here's how we did it:

As part of my estate planning, I set up a trust (a "trust" is a legal entity into which you can transfer property or assets for the benefit of other people) shortly before I retired. The particular kind of trust I created is called a Charitable Remainder Trust (CRT), and I transferred my shares of company stock into it before selling them to my children. That was important because if I had simply sold my stock to them directly, I would have incurred a large capital gain (that is, I would have made a large profit, since the value of the stock had increased drastically through the years), and, after paying the resulting tax bill, I would have ended up with only about half the value of the shares. But by putting the stock into the CRT first, I was able to get the entire proceeds from its sale (although those funds are, of course, an asset of the trust and not a personal asset), plus I got a personal tax credit for the next three years.

When I first set up the CRT some twelve years ago, the prevailing rate of interest was 10.2 percent, so for the rest of my life I'm able to withdraw 10.2 percent of its value each year, until the funds in the CRT are depleted. Of course, I have to pay taxes on that money, but any profit that the trust accumulates is tax-free—and it's accumulated quite a bit due to some successful investing (helped greatly, I might add, by the stock market boom of the 1990s). So after more than a decade of taking out money each year, I've drawn out slightly more than the original value of the Trust... and there's still nearly half the money left!

All of this, of course, is perfectly legal, and if, at the time of my death, there are any assets left in the trust, they will go to the charity of my designation, as required by law. In the meantime, as long as I'm alive, the trust will continue to provide me with substantial annual income, and hopefully it will continue to grow too.

I have found out that good financial planning is worth its weight in gold (or chopped liver, or whatever commodity is valuable to you). People look for bargains in their approach to planning, but it really does pay to work with the best experts money can buy. I have been fortunate to be able to hire some excellent attorneys and business advisors to help me with this—and, believe me, they don't come cheap—but the turnaround from that trust alone was absolutely phenomenal. Some people don't want to set up a trust because they don't want to give up control. But I don't feel as though I lost control at all, because this trust enables me to count on a significant income for a number of years.

But that's only one aspect to the value of my business. An even bigger piece of the puzzle is the value of the real estate that my company owned. It was something I wasn't even aware of at the time, but it makes for an interesting story, so I'm going to relate it in some detail.

One morning in the mid-1980s, out of the blue, I got a phone call from a Mr. M, a customer of ours who owned a small chain of clothing stores. He said he had seen our building in Ozone Park, Queens, and he wanted to buy it. I told him, "Sorry, but I have a cutting room there and I have no plans to sell the building."

He said, "You set a price—I want to buy the building."

The building Mr. M was referring to was one that my company had purchased in the early 1970s, when we were in the throes of expansion. I told Mr. M I would think about it and talk it over with my partners. They thought it was a good idea; selling the building would allow us to move part of our operation from New York to Pennsylvania, where the taxes would be lower.

We had paid $200,000 for the building originally, and I thought this was an opportunity to possibly double our investment. In addition, I figured it would cost us $75,000 to move the cutting department to Pennsylvania. So when I called Mr. M back, I told him my price was $475,000.

He said, "You're crazy. I'm not going to pay $475,000 for that building."

I said, "Remember, I didn't want to sell the building in the first place. You were the one who called *me*. But if you don't want to buy it, you don't want to buy it."

The conversation was over. I hung up the phone and didn't think anything more about it. Two weeks later, I got a call from a real estate broker in New Jersey who said he was very interested in buying our building. Now, the head office for Mr. M's store was somewhere in New Jersey, so the first thought that went through my mind was that this guy was representing Mr. M and now he's going to try to buy our building at a better price than $475,000. I really didn't want to go around the merry-go-round, so I said to the broker, "If you're really interested in this building, my price is $750,000." I figured that would get rid of him. But he said he'd think about it and a week or so later he calls me back and says, "We're interested." So immediately I knew he wasn't representing Mr. M.

I was excited. I told my partners I thought we had a good offer, but in the middle of deliberations I got a call from another broker, this time a guy on Long Island. He says, "I saw your building in Ozone Park and I'd like to buy it." So I say to him, "$800,000." He says, "Let me think about it," and he calls me back a day or two later and says, "We're interested."

Then the guy from New Jersey calls back and says, "Let's get together on our $750,000 deal" and I said, "Sorry, there's a new price: $850,000." He calls me back a day or two later and says, "Okay, we're still interested."

So now the guy from Long Island calls again and I say, "Sorry, there's a new price: $900,000." He calls me back and says, "Okay, yeah, I think we could go that high."

Meanwhile the guy from New Jersey calls and says, "What's going on? I thought we had a deal." I say, "Sorry, new price: $950,000." He calls me back and says he can live with $950,000.

Once again I huddled with my partners. Understand, at this point it's become our main focus—we almost lost sight of the fact that we were in the business of making sleepwear. We seemed to be caught in the middle of a bidding war, and we were starting to feel confident that we could get a million dollars for the building.

But then I started thinking, if the building is worth a million to them, it's worth a million to me... and maybe I can get even more long-term if I rent it instead of selling it. So I consulted with my lawyers and accountants and we came up with a plan: I went to my partners and offered to buy their shares in the building, and they agreed. Once the paperwork was signed, the building was now owned not by the business, but by me personally. Mind you, I didn't actually pay the company a million dollars for it, because on paper the building was only worth $200,000 less twelve years' worth of depreciation, which brought it down to about $100,000.

Nonetheless, I still gave each of my partners their share based on the million-dollar value; they deserved no less.

Then I called the guy in New Jersey who had offered me $950,000, and I said, "I've decided not to sell, but how about renting the building from me instead?" By that point, I was convinced that I would be moving the cutting room anyway, because it had become apparent that the building was just too valuable to use for that purpose alone. So that's what I did: I rented the building to a big pharmacy chain. We made a deal and they signed a ten-year lease with three five-year options, all of which came with built-in rent increases. All that rental income now flows directly to a separate corporation owned by me... plus, as a commercial tenant, the pharmacy chain pays for upkeep, maintenance, insurance, the works.

All of these events occurred over a period of just six or eight weeks. The whole thing took place in the blink of an eye, because everyone was getting back to me promptly, and I got into the rhythm of it. I learned a lot from the process, including the importance of making quick decisions without lingering.

Buying the building from the company was very definitely part of my retirement planning, and the rental money it generates is still a major source of income for me. It was yet another piece of the puzzle that presented itself: It not only talked to me, it was almost screaming to me. And it was almost as if it were preordained—there I was, minding my own business, when these people came to me. A lot of things like that have happened to me during my lifetime, and I think it's because I've always been open to listening to new ideas. Even if I'm pretty sure that I'm not going to get involved in the deal being proposed, I'll still give it serious consideration. That's not to say I'm always right, but I always give it my best, based on all I know at the time, and I always trust my instincts. I've found that doing so inevitably leads to other things.

So that was the positive side of my real estate dealings. I didn't do nearly so well when it came to a property that my father had bought back in the 1950s for the construction of our first factory—a building for which he paid the princely sum of $168,000. That building is ten times the size of the one which I'm currently renting to the pharmacy chain. When I began thinking in terms of liquidating the company's assets, I made the decision to sell it to the U.S. Post Office for a lot of money.

It was the biggest mistake I ever made, because today that building is worth many, many times what I sold it for. Sure, my company made a big profit on the sale, but if I had held onto that building and rented it out instead, we would have made a lot more, and today it would be an asset worth an absolute fortune. Still, in some ways it was a good thing because it conditioned me, toughening me up by forcing me to face the fact that I'd failed to see a golden opportunity when it presented itself.

Lessons learned: The biggest mistake I made here was that I should have turned my business into a real estate company— I should have bought *both* properties from my company and then rented them to commercial enterprises. So the primary lesson is: believe in yourself, trust your instincts... but *know when to change.* Change really is all about new challenges, new approaches, new ideas. Expect change, anticipate it, and plan for it. We'll talk much more about this in the upcoming pages of this book

In terms of my company's real estate assets, the lesson I learned was that, if something is really good, and everybody wants it, it's good enough for you to hold onto. If something is in demand, there's a reason.

STRUCTURING MY COMPANY'S PENSION PLAN

A few years after I took over my father's business, we started a government-supervised pension plan for our non-union employees (the union employees had their own plan). It was set up so that I didn't have to put money in unless the company made a profit, and even then I could decide exactly how much I wanted the company to contribute. The proceeds of the fund were then divided up among our employees, based on the number of years of service and salary.

During the years when the company didn't make any money or just broke even, we didn't kick in anything. But when we made a lot of money—and there were years when we made more than a million dollars in profit—I took several hundred thousand dollars and put it into the plan. As an incentive, there were no taxes to be paid on those funds, so it was a way to build up money tax-free.

When I retired after 45 years of service with my company, I had accumulated a pretty hefty pension, which I then rolled over into an IRA (Individual Retirement Account). In each of the ten years since I've retired, I've taken nothing more than the annual minimum, which is a good chunk of change... and there's still a lot more left in the IRA.

Thankfully, these are really excess funds to me, so I've made arrangements that will allow my pension to benefit my grandchildren. When I die, anything that's left in the IRA will go to them. As a bonus, I've been able to add 63 years to the life of the IRA, because that's the difference between my age and the age of my oldest grandchild. So instead of my being able to draw on those assets for the ten or twenty years I have remaining, they will be able to draw on it for 63 years. That's fine with me; as much as I love life, I don't plan on sticking around another 63 years!

Lessons learned: Find an advisor who is trustworthy, smart, and flexible, someone who stays on top of the changing tax laws. If your employer offers a pension plan, buy into it. Even if it isn't much, and even if you don't end up needing the money yourself, it can be a wonderful gift you can give to your children and grandchildren.

STOCKS AND BONDS

The purchase of a diversified portfolio of stocks and bonds was actually the final component in my retirement plan, even though for many people it's the first thing they think of when starting to invest.

There's a very good reason why I waited so long: I knew I wasn't smart enough.

During my formative years in business, when I was first learning how to sell, I watched how my father and his friends dabbled in the stock market. I soon realized that none of them really understood what they were doing—not even someone as bright and intuitive as my father. As an example, he had bought a thousand shares in Western Union many years previously at $12 a share. It eventually went up to the high 80s, but he was convinced it was going to hit 100, at which point he was planning to sell. Good plan... in theory. The problem was, long before it got to 100 (and I'm not sure it *ever* got there), it hit 8. Those were the kind of things that made me wary of the stock market. It seemed to me that it was like going to the track: you might as well randomly pick out the sixth horse in the sixth race. So when I looked at my financial future, I realized that no matter how much I knew, it would likely not be enough to beat the odds that Wall Street was giving.

There was another reason I put off investing in stocks and bonds: I was enjoying myself too much doing all the other things I've described. They got my juices flowing, and even if they weren't going well, what the heck, I was meeting interesting people, having fun, and learning new things. I was involved in all my investments, so, win or lose, they occupied my time and made me feel good about myself. As long as I understood what was going on, and as long as I had a feeling for it, it was a pleasure.

That's one of the things I really dislike about the stock market: you don't necessarily know what's going on behind the scenes. There are all kinds of faceless people doing who knows what in the privacy of their offices and boardrooms. And, as we have learned, some corporate executives lie; Enron is the best example of that. They tell the investment firms and Wall Street analysts what they want to hear, they make the numbers come out. It's called Finagle's Constant: changing the universe to fit the equation. Whatever you want, I'll give it to you. You want to be seven feet tall? You want to weigh 110 pounds? You want to see a billion dollar profit? There it is, right there on that sheet of paper. You can take it to the bank... maybe.

Let's not forget that some of the wealthiest people around—Warren Buffett excluded—opt to stay away from the stock market. John D. Rockefeller didn't believe in the market; he bought businesses, not stocks in them. Andrew Carnegie advised putting all your eggs in one basket and watching the basket. I'm saying, "Don't put them in one basket; put them in ten baskets. And make sure you watch *all* the baskets." But in the stock market, you have no chance of watching all the baskets—there will always be things going on that you don't see, don't know about, and can't control.

Frankly, I've never been too crazy about bonds, either, even though they are usually a safer bet than stocks. The downside is that there is commensurately less return. Often bonds don't do much better than inflation, and if you are investing in something that doesn't keep pace with inflation, it's like trying to fill a bathtub with a slow leak—you can't possibly succeed in the long run.

To my way of thinking, the purchase of stocks and bonds should represent only one aspect of a sound investment strategy... and I don't think anyone should get into it until or unless they have accumulated sufficient experience and knowledge, or until or unless they locate the right financial advisor, someone they can completely trust. That's why I recommend that you start with other things—things you know and can control. Don't go into the market until you've got all those other things sorted away, and until you've accumulated some discretionary funds—money you're willing to say goodbye to.

There's no denying that there is potential for doing well from the right stock investments, but you need to be willing to spend several hours every day studying and analyzing companies. You need to be prepared to stick with it for the long haul—not just jump in and out—and you need to think globally, not just locally. You need to not only know where a company has been, but where it is going, just as you have to understand both the financial strength of the company and where the potential pitfalls lie. You need to read prospectuses all the way through and you need to know something about the management personnel and their vision for the company. In the technological world we're living in today, some of the biggest companies in the world can be weakened substantially by not seeing the changes that lie ahead. That's one of the problems with a big company in particular— they're often slow to change: it's like turning a herd of elephants around. In fact, the bigger the company, the slower the change, and the more costly the change.

The good news is that it's easier today than ever before to find out about businesses you might want to invest in or even partner with. Websites provide huge amounts of information, and email allows you direct and instant contact with whoever you want to communicate. You can even hop on a plane and visit businesses directly or attend stockholder meetings and see for yourself what's going on—something you really couldn't have readily done just fifty years ago.

If you do decide to dip a toe or two into the market, there are a couple of tips I'd like to pass along. First of all, if the investment firm or stockbroker you're dealing with tries to tell you what to do, as opposed to listening to what *you* want to do, that's a sure warning sign that they are more concerned with protecting their own interests than yours, so get rid of them. Fast.

Secondly, it's just as important to look at the *volume* of shares being traded as it is to look at the *value* of the shares. If you buy stock in a very small company with just a few million outstanding shares, even if it goes up substantially, when you go to sell it, you might not be able to find a buyer. If there are only a certain amount of people who buy and sell that stock, your broker won't be able to get you full value for it, because there just isn't enough demand. So with a small company in particular, you can easily be fooled as to what the true value is.

For most of my life, I was a risk-taker. Many of the investments I made actually had more risk than the stock market itself, but I was following my heart and my passion, and for the most part I did pretty well. However, the jury is still out as to whether or not I will succeed in the stocks and bonds aspect of my retirement planning. I rode the boom of the 1990s all the way into the stratosphere... but then I made the mistake of riding it all the way down again. There's more than a kernel of truth to the old saying about how, in the stock market, sometimes the bulls are winners and sometimes the bears are winners... but the pigs are always losers.

Lessons learned: When you don't know what you're doing, don't do it. It's too easy to get fooled by your own success, and to give in to greed. That's the principle that allows both Wall Street and gambling casinos to make money. They actually aren't all that different... except the food is better in Vegas!

CREATING YOUR OWN PLAN

It should be apparent by now that not every investment I made was a lucrative one, or even a smart one. There are at least as many losers as there are winners; however, the returns I got on my winning investments were more than enough to offset the losses I suffered... and then some.

Frankly, even the losing investments were valuable, because I learned so much from them. In retrospect, they helped me see things clearly—perhaps even more clearly than the investments that were successful. Knowledge *is* power, and I hope that, armed with the knowledge you glean from my experiences (both positive and negative) you will be able to formulate a personalized plan—one that fits *your* experience and life goals, and one that is every bit as profitable as mine was.

Just remember: whether you do things in a more modest or more elaborate way than I did is irrelevant. The important thing is that you follow your passion. We'll be talking a lot more about that in the pages ahead.

CHAPTER THREE

MARRYING TIME
TO MONEY

"Chop your own wood, and it will warm you twice."
—Henry Ford

IN THE LAST CHAPTER, I talked about the epiphany I had at
the very beginning of my retirement planning when I came
up with the concept of marrying time to money. I soon became
obsessed, literally obsessed, with that thought.

I'd like you to become obsessed with it too, at least a little bit.
Trust me, it's a healthy obsession. And if you don't take anything else
from this book, take that idea and embed it in your mind, stencil it
on your forehead, brand it on your behind... do whatever it is you
have to do to make it the central focus of your own planning.

The point is that if you don't accumulate sufficient assets,
you won't survive retirement financially... but if you don't have
something worthwhile to occupy your time, you won't survive it
mentally or emotionally, which is actually far worse. Marrying
time to money successfully solves both problems and gives you
the best of both worlds.

The key word here is *passion*. Don't invest in anything that you
aren't passionate about. Just making an investment for the sake

of an investment isn't fulfilling. It may work out financially, but that would be sheer luck. Much better to invest in something you know about, something you believe in, because even if it doesn't earn money for you, it will enrich your life in other ways.

Think of it this way: If you love chopping wood, you'll get satisfaction both from the physical activity itself, and from the warmth the wood will bring you in front of a fire on a cold winter morning. Similarly, if you love collecting stamps, you'll get pleasure both from the wheeling and dealing that's required to acquire the stamps you want, and from their (hopefully) increased value when it comes time to sell them years from now. If you have a passion for cooking, invest in a local restaurant; you'll enjoy being involved in menu-planning and other aspects of the business, you'll learn from your chef, and if you and your partners are good enough at what you are doing, you'll turn a profit too.

Whatever it is you love, pursue it. Pursue it wholeheartedly, but with a clear sense of your goals, your tolerance for risk, and your own abilities and limitations. (We'll look more closely at each of these factors in upcoming chapters.) And if your interests change, or if your instincts tell you to shift gears, adjust accordingly. *Don't be afraid of change: accept it. Don't be afraid of failure: it's part of success.* And never, ever lose sight of who you are and what it is you love doing.

If you look back at the twelve components of my retirement plan, ten of them were investments in areas of my expertise (the Michigan apparel stores, the swimsuit business, the sweater business, and the pension plan I set up for my business), or in either longstanding or newly discovered hobbies (the stamp business and collecting Faberge, gold coins, art, and artifacts). By the time I got around to investing in the stock market, I even developed some interest there, at least in terms of creating and maintaining a diversified portfolio, often buying shares in businesses I knew something about. Most importantly, I had some degree of control in all ten investments. (True, I couldn't control whether the stock market went up or down, but at least I could freely choose which stocks to invest in and when to sell them.)

But there were two components that were in areas that I knew nothing about, had no control over, and had no passion for—I simply went into them out of greed. (I'm only human and sometimes even *I* don't follow my own advice!) Those were my two real estate investments (the chain of drugstores in Florida and the tax shelters), and they were both unmitigated disasters. Coincidence? I think not. Not only did I lose money on both deals—a lot of money—but neither of them were the least bit fulfilling, nor did they occupy my time productively. If I'd at least gotten some pleasure out of those investments along the way, the losses wouldn't have been quite so hard to swallow.

Freedom Is Everything

Accumulating sufficient assets for your retirement buys you the one thing that's essential: *freedom*. In fact, it buys all kinds of freedoms: the freedom to do what you want, the freedom to make mistakes, the freedom to take your time and get the most out of life.

When I was 39 and I witnessed the near-demise of my father's business, it dawned on me that what takes years to build, you can lose in the blink of an eye—and that's applicable to every aspect of life. That was the point at which I said to myself, I don't know how long I'm going to live, but I'm not going to live without my freedom. Every American should be thankful that we live in a country that allows us to pursue our dreams. Go to almost any Third World or totalitarian country and you find out what freedom is worth: it's priceless.

Throughout the years, I've seen a lot of relatives and friends struggling as they got older. It wasn't just that they suffered from lack of money; they were suffering from loss of freedom. It was a double whammy: they had nothing to do and not enough money to do anything. Don't fall into that trap. It's no way to live. In fact, you could make the argument that it's *not* living—it's simply existing. Is that how you want to spend the next thirty or forty years of your life? I sincerely hope not.

WHAT YOUR FINANCIAL ADVISER WON'T TELL YOU

There are plenty of investment firms out there that are vying for your money. They claim to employ hundreds if not thousands of experts who will look after your assets as if they were their own and grow them into a small fortune by the time you sprout that first gray hair. They make lots of promises and it is entirely possible that they can make money for you—it can and does happen.

But none of the retirement plans offered by financial institutions that I've seen make any consideration for *time*. They only address the issue of money—they try to ensure that you'll have enough money to live on after you're no longer working. But what do you do with your time? Even if their investment schemes make you big money, what do you do—just sit around and look at your monthly statements? Will your life simply become a routine of depositing the checks they send you and then you eat and you sleep? You have to have more to do than just sitting around wondering whether your money is going up or down. That doesn't sound like much fun to me.

Well, what's wrong with just taking a long vacation?, you

may be saying. Nothing. But what do you do when you return home? Watch TV? Play a few rounds of golf? If you're like most people I know, you'll tire of either activity quickly.

One thing I am certain of is that *purpose* in life, food for life, can only be attained through focused activities—in other words, by doing things that you want to do. And nowhere in any of the formal financial plans that I've seen is there provision for people investing in things they know, things they can control, things they love, in order to make money. There's no concept of marrying time to money, where people take things that they are passionate about and turn them into money-making propositions.

To survive your retirement mentally, you need to find something you love and stay busy doing it. Keep meeting new people, keep maintaining contacts, and at the same time make yourself a couple of dollars. Truth be told, these financial institutions really want to discourage you from doing that because they want you to take 100% of your assets and hand it to them, leaving you nothing to pursue other interests. The bottom line is that if you're planning on living a long and rewarding life after retirement, you can't just follow the conventional routes.

INVEST IN YOURSELF

As you'll soon see, when you're deciding on investments, diversification is crucial. Nonetheless, I would recommend that you invest a good chunk of your assets—perhaps even as much as half of them—in your dreams and your passions. This is especially true if you've enjoyed success in your life, if you feel good about yourself and are confident in your abilities. On the other hand, if you've made a lot of professional mistakes over the course of time, or if you're gullible or easily sold, or if you suffer from a lack of confidence, you might want to be more cautious and invest a bit less in yourself.

Either way, try to identify those things you love, and try to find creative ways to invest at least some of your money into those activities. If reading books is your favorite thing to do, travel around to some rare book stores and antiquarian shops and begin buying first editions. If you're a baseball fan, start attending autograph shows and invest in some signed baseball cards. If you love wandering around art museums, buy a few paintings that speak to you; even if they're from a local unknown artist, who knows? They might increase in value over time, and even if they don't, you'll have the pleasure of seeing them up on your wall. If you enjoy spending time online surfing the Internet, consider starting an eBay business, buying and selling Civil War memorabilia, movie posters, hobby horses, musical instruments, soda bottles, buttons, bows, nuts, bolts, grommets, or widgets—whatever turns you on.

Everyone has things they are passionate about, and everyone has things they are knowledgable about. Figure out what they are, put your money where your mouth is, and even if you end up losing part of that money, you will have spent your time productively and you will feel fulfilled.

CAN'T BUY ME LOVE

It's true that money can't buy love... or happiness. But money is like grease: it makes the wheels turn more smoothly. Used properly, money can *enrich* happiness. It can secure your independence, ensuring that you won't ever need help from anyone. As an important corollary, it also ensures that you won't ever have to be answerable to anyone.

Money can also buy time and opportunity to do the things you enjoy most... and it can free you from the fear of making mistakes. After all, if you have sufficient assets and you make a mistake which costs you X dollars, it's no big deal; as long as it's only a small percentage of your assets, so be it, and don't look back.

Money can also buy peace of mind, in the form of sufficient insurance, better quality healthcare, and a safe and secure home. It can help us fulfill our obligations as parents to children and as children to parents. We all want the best for our family, and having enough money allows you to provide them with many comforts. Of course, material possessions are no substitute for love and emotional support, but there's no question that being able to pay for your child's college education and for an aging parent's health care can enhance their lives significantly... and at the same time make you feel good about helping those you love.

But money on its own means nothing. If you don't believe me, ask any rich person who faces health issues or who can't engage in a meaningful relationship or who has nothing or no one to live for.

Better to have it all: financial security *and* an enthusiasm for life. And you *can* have it all. Marrying time to money is the best way I know to achieve that.

CHAPTER FOUR

BEING HONEST WITH YOURSELF

"Whatever games are played with us,
we must play no games with ourselves."
—*Ralph Waldo Emerson*

B
Y THE TIME I WAS A TODDLER, I had already made up my mind that my mother's older brother Jack was my favorite uncle. He was very likable, very gregarious, but for some reason never had a regular job. Instead, he had become a delivery man for his sister Celia's lamp business—this was, of course, back in the pre-Fedex days, so it was all by foot (or bus), not by car or by airplane. As he went on his rounds throughout our Brooklyn neighborhood, delivering lamps to local housewives, he would sell Irish Sweepstakes tickets as a sideline. As I remember it, there were twelve tickets in a book—ten tickets that were sold for about a buck apiece, and another two tickets that were a perk for the salesman; he didn't get paid, but he got those two free tickets for every book he sold. Because my uncle had the gift of gab and was constantly running all over town, he sold a lot of books, so he always had plenty of free tickets which he would assign to

everybody in the family: his mother got some, his father got some, and of course his sister and brother-in-law (my father) got some.

Lo and behold, in 1936, my father learned that the number on one of the free tickets he had been given had been selected, making the ticket worth at least $3,750—a lot of money at the time. But it was potentially a lot more valuable because Irish Sweepstakes tickets were not only numbered but they were also linked to the winnings (if any) of a horse in an upcoming race. This particular ticket was assigned to a horse named Blue Shirt, running in the English Derby.

As it happened, Blue Shirt was the favorite horse in the race, and it was listed at 4 to 1, which meant that if he won, my father's winnings would increase to a staggering $150,000. (Even if Blue Shirt came in second or third—"place" or "show," in the vernacular—my father stood to win extra money.) But there was an English bookie by the name of Friedman who had come to the United States with the intention of buying as many winning Sweepstakes tickets as he could get his hands on. He'd locate the ticketholders and offer to buy part or all of their ticket, based on the odds of the horse they were assigned to: a ticket listing a 100 to 1 horse, for example, would get less money than one listing a 4 to 1 horse. He offered my father $7,500 for a half share in the ticket, so that win or lose, my father would get $7,500 from Mr. Friedman plus the $3,750 from the Irish government. Of course, if Blue Shirt won, my father would have gotten only half the purse—in this case, $75,000, instead of the $150,000 he stood to win. But getting guaranteed money seemed like a good deal to my father—an insurance policy, if you will—so he accepted Friedman's offer.

Unfortunately, on the day of the race it rained in England, and Blue Shirt was not a mudder; he ran such a bad race that he may in fact still be running today. The horse that won—his name was Battleship—was owned by the famous actor Randolph Scott. Nonetheless, my father was now $11,250 richer.

Using the Consumer Price Index (CPI) as a measure, $11,250 in 1936 would buy you about what $170,000 can today. At the time he won this money, my father had two young sons (I was ten; my brother Arnold was eight; and my youngest brother Sam would be arriving shortly) and worked as a pattern maker and fabric cutter for a garment manufacturer in New York City. His was a skilled job, but the pay was modest so we lived a decidedly lower-middle class lifestyle.

Put yourself in his position. What would you do if you suddenly received a windfall of $170,000? Most people, I think, would buy a house or pay off an existing mortgage. Perhaps they'd treat themselves to a new car first, or a vacation, or some material things like jewelry or electronic equipment.

My father decided instead to invest the money in himself. Upon learning that his boss was planning to start up a new company—a business that would be manufacturing children's underwear—he used the money to buy a partnership. In the quaint vernacular of the day the new company was going to be named Style Undies, and such was my father's unshakeable belief in his own abilities that he gambled everything he had on making it a success.

For the next thirty years, my father gave Style Undies everything he had—blood, sweat, and tears included. Through a combination of hard work and trusting his instincts, he was able to parlay that $11,250 into a successful business which not only supported his family, but that of hundreds of his employees, touching the lives of thousands of people in the process. Was he lucky? To be sure.

But more importantly, my father knew himself. And that's really what made all the difference.

To Thine Own Self Be True

There are some people who believe they're wrong all the time. They're called pessimists. Then there are people who believe they're right all the time.

They're called delusional.

Most people are somewhere in the middle: sometimes they make very good decisions for themselves, and other times they make very bad decisions. The important thing is to know what to do with a good decision... and to be able to realize when you've made a bad decision and change direction accordingly. The action afterwards is almost as important as the decision itself.

Life has taught me that good decisions, made on the basis of good feelings, almost always result in good consequences. Conversely, bad decisions, made on the basis of misguided feelings or incomplete information, often result in bad consequences. In other words, good builds on good, while bad builds on bad. As you get closer and closer to retirement, it becomes ever more critical that you make good decisions, yet ironically it can become harder to do so because of all the pressures that come to bear, and because of fear of the unknown.

The biggest problem with making bad decisions is that you begin to lose faith in your own judgement so a kind of inertia sets in. To fight that, you need to learn from the bad decisions you make and then move on. Let it go; don't hang onto mistakes and keep blaming yourself. Remember, you're only human.

Part of knowing yourself, part of being honest with yourself, is understanding whether or not you're capable of making tough decisions and living with the consequences afterwards. I once had to fire eight hundred people in a single day. It wasn't easy to do; in fact, it was incredibly difficult. People have sometimes asked me how I managed to get through it. The simple answer is, I had no choice—either their jobs were terminated or the entire company would go under and even *more* people would be out of work. When you have to do something like that, you learn how to do it in a compassionate way, in a way that lets people know you value them. But there are some people who couldn't handle such a distasteful task, no matter what the circumstance, people who avoid confrontation at all costs; they never want to do anything to rock the boat, they're fearful of hurting anyone's feelings. That's fine; there's nothing wrong with that... as long as they recognize that limitation in themselves.

Sadly, there are even people who spend an entire lifetime wandering from task to task with no end goal in sight. They get up in the morning and they exist...and that's the way they live until they die. If they're happy in that, they're lucky, but the problem is, if you don't have any goals, you have no hope of achieving anything.

No matter your personality type, I'm a firm believer that you should never let other people make decisions for you. The only way to attain true self-worth and self-confidence is to be in control of your own destiny. It's only by making your own decisions in the course of your life that you'll know whether you're successful or not... and success builds on itself. But if you don't make your own decisions—if you let other people, even people whose opinions you respect, make them for you—you'll never really know if you can succeed on your own.

Make no mistake about it: gaining self-confidence takes practice. Everyone makes dozens of decisions every day, about what to wear, where to go, what to eat. These are really no different from decisions about buying a building, keeping a building, buying gold, selling gold—they're just on a different level. The point is that the more decisions you make, the more you'll be able to prove to yourself that you have the right stuff to succeed. That's vital psychologically because if you're unsure of yourself, if you're operating from a position of fear and uncertainty, it's almost impossible to achieve success. And you can never have true self-assurance unless you know exactly who you are.

STRIKING A BALANCE

Whatever you do in any aspect of life—choosing a mate, running a business, planning for retirement—you have to be honest with yourself.

If you don't recognize your own strengths and weaknesses, if you deceive yourself into thinking that you're something you're not, that's the surest way to make mistakes. Telling yourself "I'm going to climb Mount Everest with one hand tied behind my back this morning" isn't going to gain you anything but frustration. If you think you can do anything and everything, not only are you setting yourself up for disappointment, you're dooming yourself to failure, because no one can possibly succeed all the time, and not every opportunity is worth pursuing.

Conversely, you may be haunted with a sense that you're worthless, that you can't accomplish anything at all. You may look back on your life and feel that you haven't done much with it, so you give up, thinking "Why should I even try?" That's even more counterproductive. But either extreme—unrealistically positive or unremittingly negative—is destructive.

By the time I began my retirement planning, I had a pretty good sense of my strengths and limitations, and I knew that I had it in me to make a business work. That's why I was able to confidently go forward with the restructuring of my company's pension plan and several other aspects of my retirement planning: the stamp company, the Michigan apparel stores, the swimsuit company, and the sweater company.

On the other hand, I was in way over my head in the two real estate ventures I got into (the chain of drugstores in Florida and the New York real estate tax shelters), and both of them were big, big losers for me.

When it came to buying Faberge, gold, and art objects, I had an innate sense that I would succeed—not just because of the experts whose advice I was following, but because of an inner voice that was saying, "You have good taste." That self-confidence is what enabled me to go forward and invest relatively large amounts of money in relatively small objects. Fortunately, they were objects that increased in value tremendously over the years... which helped further reinforce my self-worth. We'll talk more about the importance of having a positive attitude later in this chapter.

As I've said, whatever plan you come up with must be customized to you as an individual, and to your passions. Passion is essential, by the way, both for the things you like as well as the things you *dis*like. If you allow your passions to dictate both the paths to follow and the ones to avoid, you have a much better chance of succeeding.

So ask yourself: What are the things during your working career that you have enjoyed the most? Those are the things that you should try to incorporate into your late-life plan. But also ask yourself, what are the things that bother you the most? Those are the things you shouldn't fool with.

William Shakespeare said it best, a long time ago: *To thine own self be true.* Those really are words to live by.

SELF-ASSESSMENT TOOLS

It isn't all that easy to do an accurate self-assessment, and it often takes many years to get to the point where you can see yourself clearly.

I'm no exception. When I first started working for my father—a man who was highly energetic, highly motivated, and highly enthusiastic—I was never quite sure if it was he that was successful and I was just along for the ride, or whether I was actually part of the reason for the company's success. That's what I had to find out, and I didn't know for sure until he turned the business over to me and I had to stand on my own two feet. It was a tough lesson to learn, but it was essential.

As you look towards the future, you need to sit down and ask yourself some very important questions. The answers will determine the paths you take in the later stages of your life, and will guide you in the planning for those years.

Here are twenty-eight questions I suggest you ask yourself as you begin your self-assessment:

1. *How old are you?*

2. *How long did your parents live? Your siblings?*

3. *How active are you relative to other people your age?*

4. *How good is your overall health relative to other people your age?*

5. *Do you have sufficient medical coverage? Long-term disability insurance?*

6. *What's your level of education?*

7. *How much importance do you place on education?*

8. *How much of a passion do you have for learning?*

9. *What hobbies do you have?*

10. *What are your main interests?*

11. *What is your job, or your main area of expertise? What jobs have you held?*

12. *What are/were your responsibilities in those jobs?*

13. *What were the things you loved about those jobs? What were the things you hated about those jobs?*

14. *Are you married? If not, do you plan on getting married?*

15. *Do you have any children? How many? How old are they?*

16. *If you have children, are they self-sufficient? If they're not currently self-sufficient, do you think they will be by the time you retire?*

17. *Approximately how much monthly income can you count on receiving in your retirement years?*

18. *Do you own your own home or condo?*

19. *What are your assets? (i.e., real estate, stocks, bonds, savings, business, car, etc.) Add them up and calculate your gross worth.*

20. *Which of your assets are liquid? (That is, which of your assets can easily and quickly be converted to cash if needed?)*

21. *What are your major financial obligations? (i.e., mortgage, etc.) Will they continue into your retirement years? Add them up and subtract that amount from your gross worth (the value of your assets) to calculate your net worth.*

22. *Where do you live? Where have you lived? Where would you like to live in your retirement years?*

23. *Do you consider yourself an optimist, a pessimist, or a realist?*

24. *Do you consider yourself a good planner?*

25. *Do you follow through?*

26. *Are you a risk-taker, or are you risk-averse? If you are married, is your spouse a risk-taker, or is he/she risk-averse?*

27. *Are you uncomfortable with making decisions, or with confrontation?*

28. *How do you react to bad news? How do you handle frustration?*

These are vital questions to ask before you start your

retirement planning in earnest, so it's well worth sitting down with a pen and paper and writing down your answers. Do it when you are alone so you won't feel self-conscious and do it when you have plenty of time, with nothing to distract you. And above all, as you answer these questions, *be honest with yourself.*

Remember, in life, the person who asks the right questions goes far...but the person who demands the answers runs the show.

SETTING REALISTIC GOALS

It was Yogi Berra who once famously said, "You got to be careful if you don't know where you're going, because you might not get there."

Actually, he had a point.

Everyone should have goals in life, dreams to pursue, but if you don't set realistic, attainable goals for yourself, the resulting frustration and your overriding sense of failure will be your greatest obstacle to success.

In my opinion, these goals should be determined by the following seven factors:

1. Your talent and knowledge
2. Your experience
3. Your energy level
4. Your degree of passion
5. Your sense of responsibility
6. The contacts you have in your network
7. The amount of risk you're prepared to take

Personal goals are important, but I don't think you should set *too* many of them, either. You've got to keep your plan down to a manageable three to five things that you want to accomplish, things that you feel you *can* reasonably accomplish. Even ten is too many, because most people can't cope with juggling that many projects simultaneously. It really takes a toll mentally and emotionally—and don't forget, you want to go out and enjoy your life while you're doing this. It's important that your state of mind, your overall attitude, remains positive at all times, and trying to take on more than you can handle can only lead to frustration.

The setting of goals occurs over an entire lifetime. It's a process that starts in school, at a very young age, and you keep building on it. Setting goals isn't just a conscious process, either; in fact, people do it all the time, often unknowingly. They set them in their interpersonal relationships with their spouse or boss and in terms of their friendships—everyone has goals about the making and keeping of relationships and the way you want people to feel towards you.

In setting your personal goals, it's vital that you be willing to face reality, but that leads to an interesting question: Is it better to aim high and know you may not get there, or to keep your goals modest and easily achievable?

In my case I reached for the stars, and it worked. I recognize that this approach won't work for everybody, but I honestly think that's the best way to go... *if* you can face the prospect of failure calmly and with equanimity. That way, even if you only come up halfway, you'll be okay with it. On the other hand, if you tend to beat up on yourself when you don't achieve what you hoped for, you probably should keep your goals modest. It's really a matter of knowing yourself well—specifically, knowing how you'll cope if you swing for the fences and strike out instead.

Is it possible to manifest success? Not necessarily, but as we'll be discussing later in this chapter, there's no question in my mind that a positive attitude plays a huge role. What's more, I'm convinced that success feeds on itself. It's like a self-fulfilling prophecy: the more successes you have in achieving your goals—big ones and small—the more successes will come your way. Conversely, if you feel that everything is going wrong, everything will go wrong. The more you get down on yourself, the more you'll be kept down.

THE FOUR-MINUTE MILE

Some years ago, my wife Carole and I were invited to attend a conference on aging in Paris that included 1,500 of the most prestigious experts in the field, including Elie Weisel, who delivered the keynote speech. It was there that I learned the surprising fact that the most critical factor to longevity is not genetics.

It's attitude.

People can live incredibly successful lives simply by having the right attitude. To gain that attitude, you have to be willing to push yourself constantly without ever backing down or giving up. You have to believe in the certainty that good things are out there—all you have to do is find them. If you don't find them today, you'll find them tomorrow; if not tomorrow, the next day. Just keep swinging the bat and eventually you'll hit a home run. And when things don't work out, don't ever get discouraged and say, "It's over, it can't work, I'm finished." Because the moment you think it's over, it *is* over.

Conversely, the moment you believe you *can* do something, you stand a chance of achieving even the impossible. We tend to treat our beliefs and mindsets as if they are real, so real that they have a huge influence on what we attempt or choose not to attempt in life. These beliefs are extraordinarily powerful in that they determine what we pay attention to and how we react to

71

difficult situations. Ultimately, they shape our attitude. The best example I can give is the story of the four-minute mile.

In 1900 the record for running the mile was a comparatively sleepy four minutes, twelve seconds. For more than half a century, no one had been able to run it in less than four minutes, and so the four-minute mile had achieved an almost mystical status— it seemed to be impossible, a physical barrier that humans could not cross. People assumed it was an insurmountable human limitation; some so-called experts believed that even if a runner *could* achieve it, his heart would explode.

But there was one man, a man named Roger Bannister, who didn't accept such thinking. An Olympian runner and medical student at England's famed Oxford University, Bannister was convinced that slow and steady training would enable him to break the four-minute mile.

On May 6, 1954, at the age of 25, he did just that. Not only had his unique training regime given him the stamina and endurance he needed, Bannister had arranged for two friends to set the pace for the first laps so he was able to complete the first three quarter-mile laps in under three minutes. Pushing himself hard, nearly collapsing at the finish line, he somehow managed to run the last lap in less than a minute too, for a final time of 3:59.4.

The "unbreakable" record had been broken.

That was impressive enough, but here's the real kicker: *Within the next three years, sixteen other runners cracked the four-minute mile.* Was there some breakthrough in human evolution that allowed them to accomplish that? No. What had changed was their thinking. Bannister had showed that it was possible.

Perception is, to a large degree, reality. *Believing* there's a limitation can sometimes *create* that limitation. Barriers that we believe are real often just exist in our minds. Sadly, these apparitions can actually stop us from achieving goals, even universal ones like finding happiness and contentment. If Roger Bannister had accepted that the four-minute mile was a physical limitation, he would have never tried to break it.

Of his own achievement, Bannister later said, "The man who can drive himself further once the effort gets painful is the man who will win."

He wasn't just talking about running, either.

Luck Is The Residue Of Design

They say that luck is the residue of design, and I believe it. Being prepared, doing your homework, calculating your risk accurately— these are the kinds of things that can improve your odds greatly.

So too can having the right attitude.

Many years ago I was in Italy on a business trip, and one morning I found myself driving from Florence to St. Tropez, with Estelle and one of my designers accompanying me. The halfway point is Monaco, along the Riviera, so we got out to have lunch. I pulled the car into the main square downtown, and we spotted a nice-looking hotel, so we parked and walked inside to their restaurant. But when I looked at the prices on the menu I nearly fainted! I said to myself, "Three hundred dollars for lunch? I'd have to be crazy to do that." But I told myself I could find a way. This being Monaco, there was, of course, a casino nearby, and 17 has always been my lucky number, so I said to my companions, "I'll tell you what: I'm going to walk inside and put ten dollars on number 17 on the roulette wheel. If it pays, it'll pay $350 at 35:1, and I'll use that money to buy lunch at the hotel; if it doesn't, we'll look for a White Castle instead."

Sure enough, I won my $350 on one spin of the wheel and we went back to the restaurant and enjoyed a sumptuous meal. The odds against that occurring, of course, were astronomical... but it happened. Was it sheer luck? Perhaps. But I'd like to think that at least a little bit of it had to do with positive attitude.

Now, I'm certainly not saying that having a good attitude is all that it takes to win money at a casino, but I have come to believe that the capability of the human mind is virtually limitless. You know what they say about mind over matter? To at least some degree it really is true, and it's not so hard to understand why. After all, everything in the universe is composed of energy—even, as Einstein proved, solid matter—and the energy coursing through your brain in the form of electrical signals is clearly affecting other things within your body. Experiments in biofeedback have already proven that humans can consciously change their skin temperature and other physiological phenomenon, just by thinking about it. There are documented cases of burn victims that have eased their suffering by focusing on mental images of ice and snow, or patients who have been operated on successfully without anaesthesia by using meditation techniques to block the pain. How hard then is it to believe that the energy in your brain can also affect things *outside* your body?

When you have a good attitude—when you feel good about yourself and the world around you—I'm convinced that these internal chemical and electrical processes can actually affect other people... and perhaps even inanimate objects as well.

Sound crazy? Consider the phenomenon called *synchronicity*, where two or more related events occur simultaneously...even though there is no cause and effect between the two (something the psychiatrist Carl Jung termed "meaningful coincidences"). For example, ever pick up the phone to call someone and hear their voice on the line even before you got a dial tone? That's something that's happened to many of us. Is it just a random occurrence? Perhaps. Or maybe somehow your thinking of calling them triggered them into thinking of calling *you*, and you both reached for the phone at the same time... even if you were physically thousands of miles apart.

There have been lots of instances of synchronicity in my life—in fact, I would estimate that it's happened to me at least a dozen times, where exactly who or what I needed appeared at just the right moment. Here's one example: Many years ago, my brother was doing the architectural work for the redesign of our Chicago showroom. I was traveling to Chicago on an early Monday morning flight and I needed to take the plans with me, so he mailed them out to me the Wednesday before (these were the days before Federal Express). That should have been plenty of time, but by Saturday they still hadn't turned up. Somehow, I had a hunch that those plans were just within reach, so on Monday, on my way to the airport, I stopped by the Post Office. It was 4:30 AM, middle of the night, and of course they weren't open yet, but the back door was ajar and so I walked in. I explained to the lone worker there that I was expecting a package and I asked if there was any way I could look for it.

"Mister," he told me, "the mail just came in—there are fifty bags of mail sitting here. If you can find it, take it."

There were a mountain of bags in front of me. One advantage I had was that I knew the plans were in a tube, so I started looking for a bag with a bulge in it. I opened the very first bag I saw that had an apparent bulge...and sure enough, there was my package, right on top.

Was that luck? Or did I make it happen that way? You tell me. So maybe luck isn't just random. Maybe the reason some people seem to be luckier than others is because they somehow know how to take advantage of seemingly random events. Perhaps that comes from pure intuition, but I don't think you're born with it—I think it's a matter of practice, of sharpening the awareness you have of the world around you and being open to new ideas.

I don't know exactly how this all works, but I do know from direct experience that the power of positive thinking *does* work, and there's no question in my mind that luck, achievement, and success all follow in the wake of self-honesty and a positive attitude.

Apply the same principles to your retirement planning, and you will indeed—in the immortal words of the *Star Trek* character Mr. Spock—live long and prosper.

CHAPTER FIVE

EMBRACING CHANGE

"Change is the law of life, and those who look only to the
past or the present are certain to miss the future."
—*John F. Kennedy*

1943 WAS A DARK TIME FOR OUR COUNTRY. We were deeply
embroiled in World War II, and nobody was really sure how
things were going to turn out. Like most patriotic young men
of the era, I prepared for service in the armed forces. I was a
student at New York University at the time, so I enrolled in
something called ASTP—an acronym for Army Specialized
Training Program, similar to ROTC. I was sent to Texas for
basic training and then shipped off to Europe, where I was
assigned to the 125th Mechanized Cavalry squadron.

I had been trained as a tank driver, but in the course of my
training I had learned that if a tank gets hit, it can explode in as
little as ten seconds. Because I was quite tall—six foot three—
I had to drive the tank with my feet hooked around the steering
levers. I knew from experience that by the time I got my legs
untangled, then managed to get up, push open the hatch,
and scramble to safety, it would take a good twenty seconds:
in other words, if the onboard ammunition were to explode,
I would be a dead man.

So when I had an opportunity to talk to the captain, I said, "I know how to drive the tank, but I also know that I'll never be able to get out in time if it gets hit. So if there's any other job you can assign me to, I'll be more than happy to do it." He replied, "I understand what you're saying. Can you handle a 50-caliber machine gun?" I assured him that I could, so he gave me a job as a halftrack gunner instead.

The next morning, when all the vehicles pulled out, the last one bringing up the rear was the halftrack, with me sitting on this big canvas tarp, manning its 50-caliber machine gun. Out of curiousity I asked the guy who was driving it, "What's in this thing, anyway?" He replied, matter-of-factly, "All the mines and dynamite." All I could do was laugh. I had obviously gone from the frying pan into the fire... but at least I was outside, on a turret, not inside the tank. Of course, if we got hit, it wouldn't have made any difference.

Our unit traveled all throughout Germany during the waning days of the war in Europe; we actually met the Russian army at the Elbe river. In June, 1945, shortly after V-E Day, I was shipped back to the United States. However, I hadn't accumulated enough points for a discharge, so Uncle Sam wasn't through with me yet. I was assigned to the Fourth Infantry Division in Raleigh, North Carolina, where we were to await orders to join the impending invasion of Japan. It was an open secret among the men that our generals were expecting 75% casualties, and I knew also that all the low-numbered divisions would be the first ones to get shipped out, because they're old army—they go back to Revolutionary War days. Because they are the divisions with the most glory, they are inevitably in the front lines... which means they inevitably get the most dangerous jobs.

I was prepared to sacrifice for my country, but I didn't especially want to lose my life, either, and I thought there was no way I'd be in the 25 percent that would survive the landing—the odds of being killed were simply too high. It was a worrying time, to be sure. Ten days later I happened to be in the office of the captain, who was complaining loudly about the buildup of mail in his office. There must have been 500 sacks of mail there, because of all the activity—people being reassigned to different outfits, people going home because they had accumulated enough points—people moving all over, with the mail chasing them. The captain was worried that if one of the general officers ever found out that all these sacks of mail were there, he'd get a lot of grief.

So I went to him and I offered to fix his problem, volunteering to work around the clock if necessary to readdress every single envelope by hand and get it out. All I asked in return is that if he got the opportunity to reassign me to a different outfit, he give me that option. He readily agreed, and so I spent the next two weeks literally working night and day, finally sending out every one of those letters. Shortly afterwards, the captain got a request asking for two tank drivers to be sent to West Point to help train cadets, and, true to his promise, he offered me the transfer. Of course, none of us knew that the top brass were already planning to drop atomic bombs on Japan and that, as a result, the war was soon going to be over. All I knew was that I was out of harm's way. So in essence I used my own initiative to save my life.

I didn't think about it at the time; in fact, I only thought about it many years later in retrospect—that I had the audacity, the chutzpah to do this. More than just a will to live, there was a readiness in me to do whatever it took to survive. I wasn't even 19 years old at that point, but I was already demonstrating a streak of independence. If I could come up with a way to improve my odds of survival, I wasn't afraid to implement it. Even at that young age

I was becoming a problem-solver—a talent that would serve me well throughout my life. There was a definite problem—namely, me possibly getting my ass blown off—and I tried to think my way around it, tried to find a solution that would still allow me to do my share, play my part in fighting the war.

Looking back, I think there's an important lesson to be learned from all this. Throughout every phase of my life, I've observed that the people who work their way through adversity tend to be successful, while the people who are frozen into inaction don't do nearly as well. They tend to hold other people responsible for their problems and failings, too, even though most of the time it's really because of their own lack of initiative. Sad but true... and a pitfall to be avoided.

CHANGE IS INEVITABLE

Why do you need to seize the initiative and be proactive in every aspect of life? For one simple reason: *Change is inevitable.* After all, nothing is linear: things don't just get better and better, or worse and worse.

They also never stay the same.

So if you don't expect change and prepare for it within the context of your own life and your own retirement planning, you're going to suffer unintended consequences, and so will your loved ones. The analogy is that if, globally, we don't begin preparing for the environmental changes which are inevitable as a byproduct of the advance of technology, all society will suffer unintended consequences.

The pace of change is accelerating too. Everything today is evolving more and more rapidly: technology, communications, transportation, health care, the size and needs of the aging population. And as one change occurs, it causes the next change in turn—one paradigm shift begets another.

Given enough information and good analytical thinking, many people can make a pretty good guess about *how* some things might change. The only thing we rarely know with certainty is *when* a particular change will occur.

What this means is that the status quo is not an option. Just as I did when I was in the military, you've got to constantly adjust and keep adjusting, and you've got to keep your eye on the horizon at all times if you hope to thrive in your retirement years. You've got to accept the need for change. In fact, you've got to embrace it.

I can't be any more blunt than this: If you don't recognize that change is intrinsic, you don't stand a chance. Unfortunately, a lot of people—even a lot of businesses—can't accept this simple and utterly basic concept. Instead, they fool themselves into thinking that things will stay the same, or that things will somehow automatically right themselves.

Tell that to the guy who made buggywhips at the turn of the twentieth century, even after the horseless carriage—the car—came into play. If he kept waiting for the horse to come back, he was in big trouble.

Or tell it to the company that keeps manufacturing dial-up modems here at the turn of the twenty-first century, or television sets that don't offer high definition, or film for non-digital cameras. If my company had simply stuck with the same fashion designs and not constantly come up with new ones, there's no way we could have lasted more than a few years.

The point is that you simply can't stick your head in the sand and think things are always going to remain as they are. Nothing does. Tastes change, styles change, people age, and no today is exactly the same as yesterday... nor will tomorrow be the same as today.

"Adapt or die" is a motto many companies have been forced to adopt since the rise of the global economy, and it's actually a good business philosophy. Look at the different approaches taken by Japanese and American car manufacturers. For years, the American manufacturers played it safe, and they also didn't focus on quality—instead, they followed the consumer-unfriendly dictum of planned obsolescence. Ultimately, that's what destroyed their reputation. The Japanese manufacturers saw their opportunity. They came in, created nice new automotive designs, put in unbelievable quality that allowed their cars to run forever, sold them at a reasonable price, and now they're the top of the heap. GM and Chrysler can say that labor costs and health care costs are what have been killing them, but the truth of the matter is that it was the people at the top, making bad decisions. If they made reliable, efficient cars, people would buy them—it's that simple.

The good news is that with endless change comes endless opportunity. You just have to be able to recognize it. Sometimes that takes thinking outside the box, sometimes it just means being able to see the forest for the trees. The signposts are actually always there... but they're not always so easy to recognize. I've known plenty of people who completely ignored signposts that were staring them in the face, causing them to not only miss a golden opportunity but failing to make the changes that would have had a huge positive impact on their lives, financially or otherwise.

One of those people, I'm sorry to say, was me. In the next chapter I'll tell you about the greatest opportunity I ever missed.

CHAPTER SIX

RECOGNIZING OPPORTUNITY

"Too many people are thinking of security instead of opportunity. They seem to be more afraid of life than death."

—*James F. Byrnes*

W HEN I RECEIVED MY HONORABLE discharge from the army in 1947, my plan was to return to school and become a doctor. Relieved to be back home, I returned to NYU, this time as a pre-med student. But the war years had been very difficult for my father's company: the priority for fabric was for military usage and certainly not for making underwear for little girls; that was really way down on the list. He had always been supportive of my academic endeavors, but with his partner's recent retirement, my father now realized he needed help and so one day he said to me, "I want you to come into the business to run the sales department." It was a rather surprising request, considering that I knew absolutely nothing about either underwear or selling at the time.

But I knew it was important to him, so I did as my father asked. After a few months of training, which was really only just enough to get me from A to B, I settled into my new job at Style Undies. To be honest, I was scared out of my wits because it was a tremendous responsibility, but my father had faith in me and served as my personal mentor. All during the war, he had sold at night; he'd come home from work and grab a quick dinner, then he'd go down to Pitkin Avenue in the East New York section of Brooklyn, trying to drum up some more business for the company. He found that he was a natural-born salesman and so was able to give me many useful tips.

At the same time, romance was in the air. My father had a very dear friend by the name of Bob Judelson, and he had a daughter named Estelle whom I had seen at a distance and was interested in. My father thought it would be a good idea if Estelle and I got together, and Mr. Judelson also thought it would be a good idea if Estelle and I got together, so he introduced us, and get together we did. We were soon inseparable, and in December, 1948 we were married. We had originally planned on a June wedding the following year... until I realized that was the busy season for Style Undies. Like the wonderful wife she would always be, Estelle was incredibly understanding, even though we had to move the wedding up six months and our guests had to face a winter blizzard instead of the summer sunshine.

A few short months after I joined the company, my father bought his partner out and became the sole proprietor of Style Undies. Its fate was now directly under his control. In some ways, it was a learning experience for him as well as for me. For example, as we were manufacturing little girl's slips—which we sold a lot of—we were cutting panties at the same time in order to get the best utilization out of the cotton fabric we were using; we may have gotten three panties for every dozen slips we cut. But nylon had just been introduced and everybody wanted it at that time because you just hung it up to dry, as opposed to cotton, which needed ironing. As a result, I simply couldn't sell them. I eventually had to go to my father and say, "Dad, we are slowly drowning in cotton panties." I think we had more than 60,000 of the damn things in stock at one point! Eventually, my father, who was very creative, came up with a different arrangement when cutting slips. Good thing he did, because we were on the verge of going broke with the world's largest supply of cotton panties on hand, but no one to buy them. In the end, we got rid of our excess stock by selling them off for peanuts.

At the time, we were leasing office and showroom space in a building on West 36th Street, in the heart of the garment district in midtown Manhattan. There were many other manufacturers in the same building, and we got to know them all. One of the companies employed a particularly talented designer whom they frequently sent to Europe for new ideas and inspiration. One year she came back with a sample of something called a bouffant dress—the puffed-out look was all the rage at the time. But in order to create the silhouette she wanted, she needed an equally puffy undergarment, and so she came to my father to help design a bouffant slip that would make her dresses stand out—both literally and figuratively. The slip he came up with, using a special combination of fabrics, was stiff as a board, but that was exactly what was required, and it became a huge hit... and we became the prime manufacturer of it, so much so that we were featured on the cover of Life magazine in 1951. After that, bouffant slips became like gold; everyone wanted one, and our sales began climbing by leaps and bounds.

The increased income flow allowed us to allocate a bigger marketing budget, which in turn gave us a higher profile. Our designers—all under the watchful eye of my father—began winning awards, and we became a leader in the field of children's underwear. Soon we were operating five plants all over Manhattan, with trucks shuttling raw materials and finished garments back and forth. Especially considering the bulk of the bouffant slip (which required a lot of space to manufacture and store), that quickly became a logistical nightmare, so the decision was made to purchase a piece of land in the outlying borough of Queens where we could construct a state-of- the-art plant that could comfortably accommodate all our new employees and allow us to fulfill the ever-growing demand for our products.

That experience gave me a wonderful insight into the determination, the fire that burned inside my father. The property we had set our sights on was going to auction, and the night before we had sat down with our lawyers and business advisers and the decision was made that the highest price we could afford was $65,000. The next day my father went to the auction on his own, and he didn't even get into the bidding until it was way over $100,000. But he wanted that piece of property and he bought it for about $120,000, nearly twice what we were originally willing to pay. Nonetheless it was a bargain, especially when you consider what real estate in New York City is worth today.

During the course of construction, I got an object lesson in trusting my instincts. We were considering hiring an architect who, acting as his own general contractor, had been building facilities for UPS all over the country and came highly recommended. In just our initial meeting, he was willing to provide a detailed costing, even though he'd only seen the property once, jotting down figures on the back of an envelope. Sometime later, I called and asked him for plans and specifications. He said, "I already gave them to you."

I said, "What do you mean? All I got was an envelope."

His reply floored me. "That's all that UPS gets, and that's all that you get."

Our attorney thought we were crazy to even think about using this guy, but my father and I had a good feeling about him so we called UPS and they confirmed that that was, indeed, all they ever got until the building was completed. There and then we decided to hire him. We thought, if it's good enough for UPS, it's good enough for us.

As it turned out, we were right. Even though every professional we consulted advised us to tack another 10 or 20 percent onto the cost estimate because things always go wrong on construction sites, this fellow actually completed the project to our complete satisfaction *under* the budget he had projected.

In 1953, my younger brother Arnold came into the business and took over the sales department while I became head of administration, finance, and marketing. Our growth rate was phenomenal. When I first joined just five years previously, there were fewer than a hundred employees; now there were more than a thousand. Despite the greatly increased numbers, my father remained a truly enlightened employer who really cared about his workers, throwing lavish Christmas parties and annual summer picnics—he even had the factory air-conditioned for their comfort, which was practically unheard of in that day and age. They loved him too, often coming to him with their personal problems and asking his advice. He treated them like family, and he viewed them that way, thus earning their loyalty and friendship. He was a wonderful role model in so many respects.

Eventually, of course, the puffy look fell out of fashion, taking with it the bouffant dress, the bouffant slip, and most of our business. We struggled to make up for the lost sales and tried everything we could think of, but to no avail. We were in such bad shape, at one point I had to fire 800 people in a single day— it was one of the hardest things I ever had to do, but there was simply no alternative. The union came in and, working together, we managed to save 90 jobs, but I still had to lay off hundreds of people. It was terrible to have to go through, but, looking back, it was a valuable learning experience. Carrying out unpleasant tasks is a necessary byproduct of taking responsibility. The best thing you can do, as I learned that day, is to tell the truth and do what you have to do in the least painful way possible.

By 1965 the writing was on the wall. Creditors were knocking on our door and we were on the verge of losing everything. One summer morning Sol Bergstein called my father and me in for an urgent conference in his office. My father walked into that meeting as the president and principal owner of Style Undies. He walked out as a retiree.

My father taught me everything he knew, and then he let me do it. Even though I was now running the business he had built from the ground up, he didn't hover over me and offer unsolicited advice; he cut me loose and let me stand on my own two feet. It was the greatest gift a father could give a son.

CHASING THE DEMOGRAPHICS

My first act as the new president of Style Undies was to cut my salary in half. In order for us to survive financially, I knew that I had to ask my employees to make sacrifices, and I couldn't do that in good conscience unless I was willing to bite the bullet too. That night, I went home, and with some trepidation told my wife Estelle what I had done. I will never forget her response. She simply said, "I'll make it work." That unequivocal support freed me to do whatever I had to do, because I knew Estelle had total confidence in me. At the same time I knew that I couldn't let her down because she was giving me everything a spouse can give.

It was a tall order. It was going to take every ounce of will—and nerve—to save the company. But I felt like I had no choice. Failure simply wasn't an option.

Instinctively, it seemed to me that Style Undies couldn't continue as it had been. We had been struggling for so long, the negativity had come to permeate the entire company, so I felt that if I really wanted to do something successful, I had to create a new corporate entity. I hired a bright young executive and put him in charge of the reorganization. He came up with a brilliant plan: we took all of the assets out of Style Undies and transferred them to a new company... but we left all of the liablilities in Style Undies. That way, the heartaches were in the old company, and the assets were in the new one, which I decided to name after my niece Jennifer Dale (the only girl in three generations of male Tolkins!).

I also offered several of my most trusted colleagues minority partnerships in the new business. In return for an eight percent stake in Jennifer Dale, they each invested a few hundred dollars, and I put in the balance—a few thousand dollars. When we finally wound down the company decades later, each partner enjoyed a huge return on his investment, so it worked out really well for them, and for me too.

As we reorganized, we were closing down some divisions and starting up some new ones, and I decided to return to selling. I knew that the only way I was going to succeed was to thoroughly understand the market... and the only way to understand the market was to go out and sell. One of my partners took the West Coast and Florida territories, and another took the East Coast. I was in charge of selling to the major chain stores and the Midwest territory, and I began traveling extensively. There was a terrific store in Rochester, Michigan that I used to enjoy visiting, and the store had a young lady who was a talented buyer. I asked her what the best-selling item in her store was and she replied, "Thermals." That's when I decided to expand our business to include thermal sleepwear for girls, and they became a big hit; up until then, only men's sleepwear had been thermal. Around this time we hired a new designer who had a fantastic eye for color. Soon we were making all kinds of print-coordinated lingerie and sleepwear: bras, bikinis, petticoats, slips, sleepshirts, robes, slippers, you name it—we went as far as our imagination would take us. It made for a wonderful presentation, and stores started to eat it up.

Shortly after returning from one of my sales trips, I asked my partners to meet with me in order to have a discussion about the future of the company and decide where we should be heading. They all felt that we should continue in the children's area because that was the market we knew. But one of my associates disagreed. He said, "Marvin, the demographics show that the teens are going to become the next big market." He was referring, of course, to the baby boomers—the kids who had been born after the end of World War II. By the mid-1960s they were becoming teenagers in large numbers, and he urged me to put our emphasis there.

Everything he said made perfect sense. I decided then and there that we needed to grow with the baby boomers, and that as our customers aged, we would age with them. In essence, we would be chasing the demographics. My partners had their doubts, but I felt strongly that I wanted us to face the future, not return to where we'd been.

Other than marrying Estelle (and, half a century later, my second wife Carole), it was the best decision I ever made in my life.

The Greatest Opportunity I Ever Missed

One of the key reasons for my success as a businessman was that I was somehow able to assimilate and analyze a problem in a very short time. People were constantly throwing problems at me—not just manufacturing difficulties like garments sewn wrong, buttons that didn't match, or looming delivery deadlines, but also personnel problems. But the more they threw at me, the faster I got at solving them—somehow, my thought processes accelerated.

It took me years to develop that ability; I certainly didn't know how to do it when I was twenty. In fact, there were lots of things that were presented to me when I was twenty that I didn't see clearly until I was sixty. I can see now that it took me a good thirty or forty years to truly realize who I was. I can honestly say that I got better acquainted—and far more comfortable—with myself between the ages of sixty and eighty than I did between the ages of twenty and sixty. That seems to be very common. I think they call it "maturing."

When Jennifer Dale faced the most basic problem any business can face—sheer survival—I was able to see that our best hope was chasing the demographic, expanding our product line to age along with the baby boomers. It succeeded beyond my wildest expectations... but that same success eventually got in my own way. It kept me preoccupied—I seemed to be doing a hundred things at once all the time—and it made me less inclined to keep advancing my thinking and move ahead on changes because there was a little voice inside me that said "Why fix it if it ain't broke?"

As a result, I became blinded to the signs that were all around me. Now, with the benefit of 20/20 hindsight, I can see that what

I should have done was to change Jennifer Dale from an apparel company to a real estate company. There was a period of time when I could have done so easily—a golden opportunity that was placed right in front of me because of someone else's failure to read the signposts, but because I was doing well, I couldn't read them either.

Here's what happened: it's a complicated story, but stick with me and I think you'll learn some valuable lessons...courtesy of my own failings.

At the very same time that Jennifer Dale was enjoying the fruits of success, my father-in-law's business was failing. For more than fifty years, he had owned an auto parts distribution company that bought from the big car manufacturers and sold to wholesalers and retailers in the New York metropolitan area—but he had failed to heed some critical signs that were foretelling disaster. The problem started when Ford, Chrysler, and GM all decided that they wanted to cut out the middle men and sell their parts directly to their dealers. Now all of a sudden there were five thousand distributors where there were once just a hundred or so in the entire country. As a result, my father-in-law was left with only the small gasoline stations and the little jobbers as customers. So the cream was taken away... and when the cream is taken away, that's the time to go.

What my father-in-law missed—and he was a bright, intelligent man—was that once that writing was on the wall, he had to think in different terms... and he didn't. The problem was that he had been in the business for so many years, he thought that things would remain that way forever. His thinking was, "Cars are here to stay, so we can't lose." But that's not true: look at General Motors. They're the biggest car company in the U.S., yet they got their brains beat out by the Japanese companies, the Germans, the Koreans. They are proof that you can be in the middle of a very successful industry and still wither on the vine.

Worse yet, once my father-in-law's business began failing, he made the classic mistake of thinking that all it needed was an infusion of capital, so he decided to sell the one big asset he had: a square block of real estate in Stamford, Connecticut, which was valued at a million dollars.

I begged him not to do it, because I was convinced that the property would be worth even more in the future, but he was desperate; he couldn't see any other way out. That's when I made my big mistake: I stood on the sidelines and watched him sell it.

Instead, I should have personally given my father-in-law a mortgage on his property. That not only would have given him the capital he needed, it would have given him some protection because if and when the worst occurred and his company failed, I would have ended up owning the property and I would have used the income it provided to help support him.

Remember, at the time I owned some real estate myself: a large building in Queens, which I ended up selling to the Post Office—another mistake—as well as another building nearby, which I rented out. I couldn't see it at the time, but the value of those two buildings alone gave me the the beginnings of what could have become a very lucrative real estate business. Instead, Jennifer Dale enjoyed some modest success as a garment manufacturer for another fourteen or fifteen years before winding down, after which I found myself the owner of one solitary building, with one single tenant providing me with income.

If only I'd seen things a little more clearly, I would have ended up owning some twenty or thirty million dollars worth of real estate, generating several million dollars a year in rent...and that's exactly what I should have done.

This was the greatest missed opportunity of my life, and it was a mistake of complacency. But it's when you get complacent that you start making mistakes. When you stand still and you don't look forward—when you rest on your laurels and ignore the fact that change is always in the air—you get into trouble.

The lesson I learned was a hard one, but it's stayed with me. My inclination had been to stay where I was, because everything was working for me... at the moment. Instead, I should have gone *outside* of where I was. You simply can't stand pat; you can't limit your thinking to only what you know. Instead, you have to make a conscious effort to think outside the box and you have to have the self-confidence to venture outside of your comfort zone; after all, that's the only way to discover new passions and develop new interests. It's not always easy, but that's what you have to do if you want to avoid missing opportunity when it presents itself.

RECOGNIZING THE SIGNPOSTS

Everybody goes through periods where their work seems nonproductive or out of phase. It happens to artists, writers, and composers all the time, and it was no different when the sales team at Jennifer Dale was picking styles to put in our line. We had years where every style we picked sold well, and then there were years when it seemed as if we couldn't come up with a single winner... even though the very same people were creating the designs and making the decisions. How could we be so right one year and so wrong the next?

Unfortunately, there is no simple answer other than that sometimes things just happen in an almost random fashion. When you find yourself in the midst of a baffling situation like that, you simply have to keep on going and work your way through the problem. You may have to fight a little harder to get yourself out of difficulty or redirect to another focus altogether, try to identify something else that you can feel passionate about. The key is to not be afraid of change. Again, *fear limits.*

I remember interviewing someone once for the job of comptroller. In the course of the interview he was telling me about his previous employer and how, due to changing market conditions, this company had slowly gone bankrupt over a long period of time. I asked him, "Why didn't you go to the owner of the company and tell him about this? You knew about these circumstances three years before the company actually went under." To my amazement, he replied, "Tell him? What do you mean?? I'd be out of a job." Of course, if he had alerted the owner as soon as he was aware of the problem, maybe he would have saved the company, and consequently would have *kept* his job. I immediately knew he wasn't the right person for me: out of fear, he had protected his own interests, and at the expense of the company that was paying his salary.

To deny the inevitability of change—particularly in terms of those things that are going to directly affect you—opens the door to a multitude of bad things occurring... and then one day you'll wake up and say, "How did this happen to me?"

A lot of people may realize this instinctively, but for one reason or another—even if they're as sharp as my father-in-law—they fail to recognize impending change even when it's staring them in the face. But the signposts are actually always there; you just have to be alert enough to see them.

I try to learn from my mistakes. Thankfully, a few years after I missed the opportunity to turn Jennifer Dale into a real estate company, I was able to successfully read a signpost that told me

I had to make a change.

Unfortunately, it was that same signpost that told me I had to begin wrapping up the business altogether.

By the mid-1980s, Jennifer Dale was doing about two million dollars a year worth of business with the retailer Bamberger's (a company owned by Macy's). One day their vice-president came to me and said, as nice as could be, "Marvin, I know that this year we're doing two million with you, but next year we're only going to do one million, and the year after, nothing. We're not going to need you because we're going to do it all ourselves—we're going overseas and we're going to make our own garments, and for a lot less money." He said it me in the same tone of voice in which he would have said "today is Tuesday." At that moment I realized that our customers were becoming our competitors.

I knew then that we were through. It was obvious that soon enough, *all* our larger customers would be going down that same path. The writing was on the wall; all that remained at that point was for me to wind things down in an orderly fashion.

I was able to do it fairly easily, too, because, relatively speaking, Jennifer Dale was a fairly small company. In many regards, that's what allowed us to adapt and shift course easily throughout our entire existence. It's extremely difficult to build a giant business and keep it going over the long term, because it becomes like an elephant plodding down a road. How easy is it to get an elephant to change direction? Those companies build up such a corporate culture, such a fixed approach to doing business, that it's often quite difficult for them to readjust to all the changes that are constantly taking place around them.

I guess it comes down to this: You need to be smart and not stubborn. You need to realize that just because you made a business work twenty years ago doesn't necessarily mean you can do it today. Author and entrepreneur Cameron Johnson summarizes the need for recognizing signposts—and reacting to them—this way: "A business owner must never fall so in love with his ideas that he/she fails to see that they are not working—or that the market is changing around him. Continue to question the validity of your original plans. Keep a list of other strategies, products, and opportunities worth exploring. Remain open to the possibility that refocusing, selling the business or shutting down might become your best option."

Of course, not everyone is a business owner; most people are workers. But there are definite signposts for workers too, indicators that tell you it's time to begin making other plans, to start thinking about moving on. One big giveaway is when your employer tells you that they can't give you any more money, that a long-overdue and deserved raise is being denied. When you see that the company is cutting back instead of expanding, it's time to begin looking elsewhere. You can also read a lot into subtle psychological signs: employees begin questioning where the company is going, or you sense a general malaise, a kind of "who cares?" attitude.

Similarly, if you see that the owner of your company is not hands-on, is not "knee deep in the mud" on a day-to-day basis, that's a sure sign of trouble. My accountant was recently telling me about a client of his, a business owner, who mentioned that he had recently won a number of golf trophies. The accountant told him, "You know, the more golf trophies you get, the sooner your company is going to disappear." Several years later the business was gone... and it was a big one, too, taking in about $300 million a year. But the owner got too involved in his golf, so it failed.

A business is like a baby: you've got to take care of it every day. You can't neglect it, you can't take extended vacations, you can't be distracted and divert your attention somewhere else.

There's no such thing as being part pregnant, and there's no such thing as partly running a company. No matter how good middle management might be, it can't be done.

Unfortunately, the trend in corporate America today is that they don't value their employees; they're always looking to replace them with someone younger, who will work at half the salary. It's fine to bring in fresh blood every now and then, but these companies don't realize that it is the older employees who have the savvy, the experience, the contacts..and the loyalty. Once they see that their loyalty isn't being reciprocated, these older, more knowledgable employees tend to move on...and more often than not take jobs with their previous employer's most fierce competitors, bringing with them important information and perspective.

The key to career longevity is to consciously stay alert to all the changing conditions that are occurring in your place of work. Keep your antenna out at all times, and take note of even the most minor shifts in attitude or company policy. You also have to accept that no matter what your company accomplished a year ago or ten years ago, it won't necessarily be able to replicate those accomplishments next year, or ten years from now. Just because things are good now is no guarantee that they will stay good forever. Look at the telephone business: a decade ago, landline phones were the only phones. Now they barely exist in some countries! Everything today is cellular. Anyone who made the mistake of investing in phone company stocks in the 1990s knows the story all too well.

OPPORTUNITY IN RETIREMENT PLANNING

Just as you can't succeed in business—any business—without anticipating change and adapting to it, neither can you succeed in retirement planning. In my case, looking for opportunity in business transferred itself to looking for opportunity in investments that would support me and fulfill me in my retirement years. And the common thread in both endeavors was that I needed to look ahead, not back.

That's the cornerstone of recognizing opportunity: *knowing where you're going, not just where you've been.*

What's more, I firmly believe that if you keep looking for opportunity, you will find it. As you gather experience in life—experience about dealing with people, about dealing with money, about trends in both local and global markets—you come to realize that you never stop learning. But it's not just about learning; it's about *using* what you've learned. It's about understanding what is going on all around you, being able to focus in on the small details without losing sight of the big picture. It's like taking a photograph with a camera: you've got to zoom in or out to get exactly the right distance in order to see the entire scene in all its clarity.

And as you do that, you have to keep yourself open to new ideas. You have to keep thinking about what is likely to happen ten years from now, twenty years from now, forty years from now. That's what I did when I told my son that I wanted us to focus on buying stamps from countries that I felt were likely to become more and more important in the years ahead. That's what I did when I invested in the newly released Chinese gold Panda coins instead of the more accepted South African Krugerrands.

Within the scope of everyone's means, I'm convinced that there are appropriate investments. Scarcity is one aspect that can be key. In the case of the Chinese gold Panda coins, for example, it's the limited amount made that keeps them valuable: there were only some 15,800 one-ounce Pandas minted when the coin was introduced in 1982, but there are 1.3 billion Chinese people and thousands of people collecting Chinese coins all over the world. It's simple mathematics—it's really not complicated.

I'm constantly reviewing everything I do in terms of what I believe to be the future. What's more, I'm constantly reexamining the future, constantly trying to look at it through different eyes. For example, given the new awareness of global warming, I see opportunities galore in the alternative energy field, especially here in the United States. A lot of today's small companies that work in that field are going to be huge companies in the future—I'm convinced of that. It's just a matter of picking *which* of those firms will succeed in the long run.

From a global viewpoint, Switzerland presents itself as the classic example of an entire country that has been affected by technology—in this case, digital watches. Of course, there are still people making watches in Switzerland, but they're making a whole lot less of them, and as a result the prices of those handmade watches are rocketing straight up.

There are new thoughts out there all the time. You simply have to find them. You won't necessarily come up with the best solution every time—you can make mistakes, you can be misguided—but the point is that you've got to keep looking. What you *can't* do is say to yourself, "I've made mistakes so I'm a failure and I'm going to give up." As we've seen, failure is a part of success—an important part. Everybody is wrong some of the time. That's what makes us human. They put erasers on pencils for a reason.

Everyone, no matter what their income level or status in life, wants to make a good life for themselves. The opportunities are out there, and if you follow your passion and keep your eyes open, I promise you, you'll find them.

CHAPTER SEVEN

UNDERSTANDING RISK

"Experience defines us, wisdom guides us,
but fear limits us."

—*Anonymous*

FOR THE FIRST FEW YEARS OF ITS EXISTENCE, Jennifer Dale was building slowly—we went from doing $3 million a year in business to $5 million a year. I had established a number of important professional relationships but our sleepwear was still not available through most major retailers—with so much competition, it was a tough nut to crack. Sears Roebuck did carry some of our lines, although our business with them was modest—really just a drop in the bucket.

One afternoon, I had an appointment with a lady named Pam, whom I had first met when she was an assistant buyer for Sears. Pam was just in her twenties but she had great instincts, and we'd developed a good professional rapport; we'd get together a couple of times a year to have lunch and write a few orders. After a few years as assistant buyer, she began to receive a number of well-deserved promotions; I heard through the grapevine that she was in line to become Sears' first female merchandiser. We had only sporadic contact while she was being groomed in their

Chicago home office, but then one day I learned that Pam had been placed in charge of buying sleepwear and underwear for the entire chain. Better yet, she was now based in New York. I immediately called and offered my congratulations and the next day we got together for lunch.

The lunch lasted six hours. Pam had brought with her one of those speckled notebooks they use in school, and it soon became obvious that she was using the opportunity to pick my brain and get a crash course in every aspect of garment manufacturing: fabric, construction, quality, costing, everything. I was happy to help, of course, but somewhere during the last half-hour I said to her, "You know, I don't mind giving you all this information but I'd also like to increase our business with Sears Roebuck if we can."

She said, "Yes, absolutely. We'll make that happen."

"Great!," I replied. "Mind you, it will take me six months to a year to ratchet my production up to be able to supply you with more sleepwear, but between now and then I'd like you to think about it."

"I definitely will," she answered.

We finished our lunch and returned to our respective offices. I had no firm committment in hand but I was willing to take the gamble of expanding and retooling based solely on Pam's new position and my longstanding business relationship with her.

But about forty-five minutes after settling behind my desk I got a phone call from her. In her usual no-nonsense way she said, "You think I'm going to wait a year for your merchandise? I want to see you and your samples in my office at nine o'clock tomorrow morning." I stammered something about production schedules, but she just repeated, "Be in my office first thing tomorrow morning." And of course I said I'd be there. No garment salesman worth his salt is going to tell a buyer at Sears Roebuck, "I'll talk to you in a year."

The next morning I showed up bright and early. Pam had a group of four or five people with her, all from different departments, and they eagerly looked over the sample garments I had brought with me. With each new piece I took out of my case, they got more excited; their enthusiasm was building on itself. When her colleagues left and we were alone, Pam said to me, "Here's what I want to do: I'm going to buy $20,000 worth of goods for each of ten stores." I thought, okay, $200,000 worth of business—that, I can handle. Then she said, "I need them all in stock by October 1," and I agreed to do that, too. Over the next few weeks, we moved heaven and earth and managed to ship everything on time. By Thanksgiving every single garment was sold. Once more I was invited to Pam's office.

This time I couldn't believe my ears. "Marvin," she said, "We've done really well with your products. Now I want you to write up an order for everything I'm going to need for the entire next season—May through October—and I want to order for 180 stores."

I gulped. The size of such an order could easily overwhelm our business... but it could also propel us into the stratosphere. Talk about taking a gamble! But I had no time to think about it. I figured, let me try to nail down the contract first and I'll worry about fulfilling it later. I spent the entire weekend writing up that order. It was a monumental task and it was very complicated because I had to break the 180 stores down into different categories, based upon their projected sales, market share, geographical location, and many other factors. On Monday morning, I returned to Pam's office, weighed down with the orders—it was the size of a phone book, because it was for 180 stores, with six separate monthly delivery orders for each store. I had to write the whole thing up by hand, too, because there were no computers at that time.

Pam took a cursory look at the book and said, "You're telling me this is what I need?"

"Yes, it is," I replied, and began explaining my thinking... but with a wave of her hand she stopped me mid-sentence. Without further ado she took a pen and signed the paperwork.

Jennifer Dale nearly doubled its entire annual business overnight with that one single order.

That one business deal—which not only changed everything in my business but in my life—was based on the simple principle of trust. Pam was taking a tremendous risk by placing so much faith in me. If I had screwed up, steered her wrong so that she ordered more garments than she could sell, or sent the wrong kinds of garments to the wrong stores at the wrong points in time, her job was probably on the line. But it was a calculated gamble she was taking: thanks to our many years of working together, she knew that I knew my business from the ground up.

It was a risk that paid big dividends for both of us. Over the coming year, every one of those garments was sold, making Jennifer Dale a substantial profit... and making Sears an even larger profit. We both got exactly what we needed out of that business transaction, which should be the goal of any successful negotiation. Over the next three years, the annual business I did with Sears went from $4 million to $8 million, representing some $18 million in sales for them.

I was 47 years old when this occurred, and I remember thinking to myself, "At last, I'm on my way." At the same time I started to think about what I was going to do with the money. That's when the retirement planning ideas in my mind began being implemented: for the first time, I had sufficient personal funds to begin investing. That was the good news.

The bad news was that I was going to have to risk that money in order to have a shot at success.

FACE YOUR FEARS

There are lots of self-help books out there that proclaim that you can do anything you set your mind to.

I've lived long enough to know that's not always true.

Sorry to burst your bubble, but we're talking reality here, not pie in the sky. Now don't get me wrong: I believe firmly that you can do *most* things you set your mind to, but only if you have a clear vision, know your own strengths and weaknesses, and, most importantly, are aware of your tolerance for risk.

Understanding risk may in fact be the single most important topic in this entire book, because if you can't accept the need for risk and the inevitability of making mistakes, you are extremely unlikely to be successful in your retirement planning. And the first step in the process is being willing to face your fears.

Cold Hard Fact #1: You cannot make big gains without being willing to take some risk. As Will Rogers used to say, "You've got to go out on a limb sometimes because that's where the fruit is."

But many people are afraid of risk. They view it as a negative, as something to be avoided at all costs. They live in fear. They spend their entire working lives doing only the bare minimum, terrified of trying something new and possibly making a mistake that might cost them their job. I've seen that even in professional buyers for major retail chains—they only want to buy things that will definitely sell sooner or later, things like plain white cotton panties. Their mindset is, "This way, my boss won't hassle me." These are people who never move forward, never make any progress in their life. They're afraid of making a career change, or of moving to a different city, even though deep down they realize that it may be the only way to find happiness and contentment. I'm always saddened when I meet people who live their lives that way.

In financial terms, these individuals (called "risk-aversive") don't really invest. Instead, they put all their money into a savings account, or a bond or CD that may not even keep pace with inflation. Their money may be safe...but it also isn't working for them, and certainly isn't growing into the support system they'll need when they retire.

But the reality is that if you don't take any risks, you generally can't accomplish much: playing it safe is simply not the way to build. Doing the same thing over and over again is usually disastrous to *any* business—look at the manufacturers who made men's hats forty years ago, or slide rules twenty years ago. Nonetheless, people tend to gravitate to the tried and true, they look to take the safe way out, and they shy away from taking chances.

Most people have to put up with being controlled by someone else for most of their lives. Up until the age of 18 or so, your parents basically control you, and from 20 to 65 it's a variation of some employer, customer, or spouse—someone else is always telling you what to do. But your retirement years provide you with the golden opportunity to finally call the shots for yourself. Don't you want to finally achieve the freedom to express your own personality? It's within your grasp, believe me... but you've got to be prepared to take some risk to get there.

Please understand: I'm not suggesting that you take unreasonable risks. Jumping off a tall building in hopes you'll survive is foolish, same as putting all your money into one basket—especially if it's a basket you don't understand and have no control over. Nor am I advising that you always ignore your fears. Fear sometimes serves a real purpose in that it heightens our awareness and brings a note of caution to what might otherwise be a disastrous behavior. It makes sense to be afraid of fire, for example, or of a bear you might encounter on a hike, or of venturing alone into a dark alley in a questionable neighborhood. There are other fears—classified as phobias—which are unwarranted and irrational. Nonetheless, the common thread is that fear is what *limits* us, not just financially, but in every aspect of life.

To overcome them, you need to face your fears head-on. In some cases, you need to follow Eleanor Roosevelt's sage advice: "Do what you fear most." Analyze them unemotionally and sweep aside any that appear to be unfounded. Once you are able to do that, you will be able to accept risk.

Then all you need to do is to make sure that the risks you take are *calculated* ones.

CALCULATE YOUR RISK

Calculating risk—that is, figuring risk versus reward— is all about knowing the right questions to ask. When you're assessing risk, you can't ask a hundred questions because then you'll overanalyze, you'll get too bogged down in minutiae. Instead, you should really only ask a few crucial questions. The important thing to know is *which* questions to ask.

Every problem has components. The way to solve a problem quickly is to identify the most important components and focus on those alone. All the other components don't mean nearly as much—you can add them in later, after you've come up with a basic solution.

So, for example, if you're trying to calculate the risk of an investment in a local business, here are some general questions you should ask (of course, there will also be a number of specific questions, depending upon the nature of the business):

1. *How big is the market for the products or services being offered by this business?*

2. *Do I understand the market?*

3. *Who will run the business?*

4. *Who is the competition?*

5. *What will be the cost to set up the business?*

6. *What are the projected markups for the products or services being offered?*

7. *What are the cash flow projections?*

8. *What is the short-term (1-3 year) and long-term (5-10 year) outlook?*

If you find the answer to all these questions satisfactory, this probably isn't too risky an investment, and you may well want to consider putting your money into the venture, even if the return is relatively modest. If the answer to most of them is satisfactory to you there's a fair bit of risk involved, but it may still be a worthwhile investment...if the potential reward is sufficient. If, on the other hand, you aren't satisfied with the answer to most of them, you probably should take a pass unless the reward being offered is significant and you have sufficient assets to offset the possible loss. And if the answer to all of them is unacceptable to you, walk on by, because this investment is probably not for you.

Similarly, here are some basic questions you should ask before investing in a particular stock:

> *1. What is the company's place in its market?*

> *2. Who is their main competition? How well are they doing?*

> *3. Who are the key management people? Do you consider them to be visionary?*

> *4. What is the company's short-term (1-3 year) and long-term (5-10 year) outlook?*

> *5. What is the company's track record? How has their past performance been?*

> *6. What is the price of the stock in relation to the profitability of the company?*

I went into almost all of my investments with a clear sense of the risk involved. The stamp business was something I knew pretty well already, and my son Larry and I did plenty of research before venturing into each new area. Ditto for buying Faberge (where I had an expert advising me), and artifacts, gold, and stocks and bonds (where I had confidence in my own taste and/or judgement). Of course, I knew the undergarment and sleepwear business like the back of my hand, so the Jennifer Dale investments were, in my view, extremely safe ones.

In the case of the Michigan apparel stores, the swimsuit company, and the sweater company, they were all in areas related to my profession, so I had a pretty good sense that they had a reasonable chance of succeeding. Unforeseen circumstances intervened, however (as they often will), and so these were investments that turned out differently than I would have hoped, but the point is that I didn't go into them with my eyes closed.

The exceptions, once again, were my two real estate investments (the chain of drugstores in Florida and the New York tax shelters). This was an area I really knew nothing about, and so the risk was essentially unknown to me. They were investments that lost me a lot of money, and they were investments I never should have made in the first place.

Oh well. You live and you learn. They say that to err is human, to forgive, divine. If I can ever stop kicking myself, I'll start forgiving myself!

Have An Exit Strategy

It's easy to get into pretty much any kind of investment, but not always so easy to get out. So before you put your money into *anything*, you'd better think about how you can get out if things take a turn for the worse. I learned that in business; it becomes instinctive, like two and two is four. You say to yourself, "I'm going to buy X, but if I end up not using it, I know exactly what to do to sell it." The idea is to ensure that you always get *something* out of whatever you invest your money in—you may not make a profit, and you may not even get all your money back, but at least you won't lose everything.

I can't stress enough how important it is to always develop an exit strategy *ahead of time*. There has to be some kind of mechanism in place that gives you a way to cut your losses, and you need to know how to exercise that option—in a hurry, if necessary—if and when the time comes to bail out. Usually, developing an exit strategy isn't too difficult; in most cases, there's already one in place. If you're buying tangible items like real estate, or gold, or stamps, you always have the option of selling them... even if you have to do so at a loss. And, of course, in today's world, there are lots of opportunities to dispose of things: you can always put them on eBay—even if it's a house!—and invariably somebody somewhere will want it... provided it's priced right. The Internet provides all kinds of ways to find out what something is worth and how to move it out if you want to get rid of it.

Not having an exit strategy can lead to disaster. One good example of that was my investment in the real estate tax shelters. I had no exit strategy because, as a limited partner, I had no real control. When it became apparent that it was a real loser and could not possibly become profitable, I couldn't sell my shares in the investment. In fact, I couldn't give them away; I didn't know what to do with them. Big, big mistake.

With non-tangible items such as stocks and bonds, you can always get rid of them, or instruct your broker to automatically get rid of them if they drop below a certain value. Then there are time-limited investments such as IRAs, fixed-period CDs, etc. It may not be immediately apparent, but there's even a way out for those kind of investments... if you're willing to take the early-withdrawal penalty. In fact, sometimes taking that penalty is the smart thing to do, because you can then do something better with the money. And don't forget, the government will share in your loss. (Any qualified tax adviser can show you how that works.)

Of course, you've got to have some idea what you're going to do with the money after you've taken the penalty; you have to know where you're going after you've cut the umbilical cord.

The point is that most of the time there's a way out... if you look hard enough. There may be a price to pay in getting out of a bad investment—even a substantial one—but there's still a way to bail and sometimes it's worth doing. Unfortunately, many people refuse to face reality, especially if it means bad news. But to succeed, you must be prepared to cut your losses the minute you get a bad feeling about it. Don't wait: waiting generally costs you *more* money. It's like any relationship—social or business: if you're not happy, if you're not satisfied, not fulfilled, walk away. Because the truth of the matter is, the longer you stay, the worse it gets.

Cold Hard Fact #2: Walking away and cutting your losses is sometimes the best option. If you have to take a beating, take the beating. Don't sit with a bad investment, because that eats at your psyche, which does you no good. Don't keep looking at it, because if you continually analyze your mistake, it can destroy you emotionally... which, believe me, is much worse than just losing money. If you keep thinking, "How stupid could I have been?" you'll start doubting yourself, and that's a tough spiral to escape from. The best thing to do is to get rid of whatever was causing you to lose the money and move on.

The lesson here is a simple one: Accept that sometimes the best way is the way out.

Know Your Limits

Investing is a little like embarking on a love affair: you always need to know how much it is you can afford to lose.

If you've ever gambled, you know the emotions: if you win some money, you feel great about yourself; if you lose some, you feel lousy. The difference is that if you lose what you were willing to lose, you can forget it quickly and move on: "Ah, so what, I had a hundred bucks to blow and I blew it." It's when you lose money you can't afford to lose that you really start beating up on yourself.

And that's dangerous territory, believe me. There's the financial loss, of course, which can be tough to bear, but much worse is the loss of self-confidence. You can't let a bad investment keep you from ever trying again. Whether you've invested your cash in a failing business or your heart in a failing romance, you've got to regroup, think through the mistakes you've made, and then go forward. After all, there's nothing worse than living as a loser—punishing yourself, every day, in a hundred different ways.

My point is this: even if you lose at times—which you inevitably will—it's important to *feel* like a winner. You need to be able to look in the mirror and tell yourself, "I feel good" every single day. Too many people shy away from getting involved in things because they'll feel badly if it doesn't work out. But you can't put yourself in a corner and simply say, "I can't do it, I'm not going to do it, I'm finished, I'm through." Again, *fear limits.*

I enjoy gambling and I go to the casino periodically. But my mindset is that I always want to walk out a winner—even if I've only won five bucks. I once won $400 on the third hand of blackjack I'd been dealt. I'd only been in the casino for ten minutes, but it so happened that at dinner earlier that evening with my designers, I'd spent just about that same amount. Knowing that our meal had just been paid for made it easy for me to simply walk away and cash in my chips, even though it put an early end to the evening.

On the other hand, if things don't go my way and I find myself on the losing end of things, as soon as I get to the point where I've lost all the money I was prepared to, I walk out. Immediately. And I never, ever feel like a loser.

So I'm just as human as the next guy and I fail frequently. How then do I manage to keep feeling like a winner?

Simple. I accept that failure is a part of success.

DON'T BE AFRAID TO FAIL

Cold Hard Fact #3: Failure is inevitable.

I hate to be the one to break the news to you, but you're going to make mistakes. No ifs, ands, or buts about it. Mistakes are part of life; they are as sure as death and taxes. Nobody steps up to the plate and hits a home run every time. Not Babe Ruth, not Mickey Mantle, not Barry Bonds. And surely not you or me.

So expect to make mistakes. Don't be thrown for a loop when you screw up; understand that making mistakes is part of the process. If you make a hundred decisions randomly, you'll get about half of them right—that's just simple statistics. But let's say you have a good analytical mind and you're really good at focusing in on the most important components. In that case you might expect that eighty or so of your decisions will be good ones. But that still means that twenty of your decisions will be bad ones. That's just the way things are; that's life. The important thing is to anticipate making mistakes and to not beat yourself up when it happens: just learn from your errors and move on. And be compassionate with yourself. The truth of the matter is, you weren't born perfect, you're not going to die perfect...and in the middle, you *aren't* perfect.

Most people would agree that the smartest man in the world during the last hundred years was Albert Einstein. He developed the Theory of Relativity that all modern physics is based on. (Please. Don't ask me to explain it to you. The only Theory of Relativity I know about involves in-laws and squabbling cousins.) But did you know that he spent the last thirty-five years of his life trying to develop a concept—something called the "Unified Field Theory"—that never panned out?

So even Einstein made a mistake—a big one. He spent nearly half his life chasing a red herring. Do you think you're smarter than Einstein? I certainly don't.

Author Daniel Levitan, in his best-selling book, *This Is Your Brain On Music*, offers this perspective:

> "... on average, successful people have had many more failures than unsuccessful people. This seems counterintuitive. How could successful people have failed more often than everyone else? Failure is unavoidable and sometimes happens randomly. *It's what you do after the failure that is important.* [italics mine] Successful people have a stick-to-it-iveness. They don't quit. From the president of FedEx to the novelist Jerzy Kozinsky, from Van Gogh to Bill Clinton to Fleetwood Mac, successful people have had many, many failures, but they learn from them and keep going."

So don't let the fear of making mistakes stop you from taking risks. After all, if you don't jump in the water, you'll never learn to swim; you'll always be on the shore, watching other people swim.

It's equally important to recover quickly from your mistakes. I spent fifty years in the garment business, and it only recently dawned on me that recovery is like the elastic in panties. When the elastic doesn't recover from being stretched, the panty is dead. The same is true in life!

The simple fact is that if you don't have confidence in yourself, if you're afraid of making mistakes, you won't give yourself a chance to make successful investments. That literally takes years to build; it's got to be reinforced over and over again. Being able to walk away from a casino after you've won a modest sum (as opposed to continuing to play with "the house money," as most people do) reinforces that confidence; it makes you feel good about yourself, it gives you assurance that you're in control of your own destiny. The money, in fact, is far less important than your feeling about yourself. If you don't have that assurance and self-confidence, then you start to play your cards too close to the vest, like you need four aces all the time. How often are you going to get dealt four aces?

As you've seen, half of the things I did in planning for my retirement failed. I made lots of mistakes, but expecting to make them and recovering from them quickly allowed me to go forward and not look back. Each failure added to my knowledge, gave me valuable experience, and, most importantly, increased my ability to adjust to change and recover.

I make plenty of mistakes because I do a lot of different things, and that increases the odds of things going wrong. In fact, I've discovered that the best way to develop a good sense of risk is by taking risks over and over again, with an end goal, a reward, in mind. Risk and reward, after all, are tied together—you could even say that they're kissing cousins.

So keep your head held high when things go wrong, as well as when they go right, and in every venture you attempt, try to follow these five basic rules:

1. *Know how much risk you're taking.*

2. *Know how much risk you're willing to take.*

3. *Know how much you stand to gain versus how much you stand to lose.*

4. *Have an exit strategy in place in order to limit your potential losses.*

5. *Don't beat yourself up when things go awry. Recover quickly and get right back in the game!*

Each risk has its own unique set of criteria: it's one thing to gamble on stocks, another to gamble on gold, or real estate. If you're taking a small risk—a few bucks here and there—it's fine to go with your gut instincts. Far better, though, to have solid knowledge. But even if you know everything there is to know about an investment, you still need to hedge your bets. That's where diversification comes in.

CHAPTER EIGHT

THE IMPORTANCE OF DIVERSIFICATION

"Money is like manure.
You have to spread it around or it smells."

—*J. Paul Getty*

THAT ONE ORDER FROM SEARS changed everything for both Jennifer Dale and for me. Within a week, I went out and bought a plant in Pennsylvania. It was a complete turnkey operation that included cutting, sewing, and finishing, and I was able to employ about 250 people there. I had that solid order in hand, and I had an obligation to fulfill it...and fulfill it we did.

But after a few years I began thinking that maybe we were doing *too* much business with Sears. With all our eggs in one basket, if for some reason we lost the account, we would be in terrible trouble. So I made the important—no, *critical*—decision to diversify. I aggressively pursued business with Sears rival JC Penney, just to protect ourselves, and soon wrote two million dollars worth of orders with them. Then everyone started hopping on the bandwagon: as they say, success begets success. Within a year, all the major retailers across the country—Montgomery

Ward, K-Mart, Macy's, and the May Company among them—were carrying our lines, and the orders were rolling in. Before I knew it, we were doing $40 million worth of business a year. It's true that I was selling to competing stores, but we weren't putting our label in all our garments—the Jennifer Dale label was only sewn into goods destined for sale at some department stores. Other lines, like the ones we developed for Sears and JC Penney, were exclusive and carried their own labels.

With all the increased success, I was sorely tempted to leave all my personal assets in the business as well. It made sense logically. The garment industry was something I loved, something I knew inside out, plus, as the owner of my company, it was something I had nearly complete control over... and business was booming. But my instincts told me to take some of the money off the table and move it around, so I did.

That can be a tough lesson for some people to learn: *follow your instincts.* You need to have a certain degree of self-confidence to go where your gut tells you, but even if you don't have that self-confidence, you should still trust those feelings more often than not. That's not to say that you should be impulsive and follow every whim that crosses your mind. But when you get a strong feeling that you should follow a certain path, it's important to listen to that inner voice and give it lots of weight in your ultimate decision-making.

In the early 1980s, that inner voice told me that in order to move forward in the business world, I had to find new areas of growth for my company. Note that I said new area*s*—plural. By this time, I had learned the value of diversification and there was no way I was going to take the extreme risk of expanding into just one new venture. Instead, I decided to go into four different areas, with the expectation that one, or perhaps two, of them might work out and become profitable.

As it turned out, I was wrong: all four of them succeeded. I put that down partly to luck (although, as we have seen, luck is often the residue of design) and partly to my knowledge of the business, which by that point was pretty extensive.

Here are the four areas I chose for expansion:

1. I made a deal with a very talented designer named Willi Smith, who had trained in New York before he found fame and fortune in Australia. When Willi returned to New York, I hired him to create designs for us in the loungewear field. They were so successful, I had to go out and buy a factory just to handle those orders!

2. Again chasing the demographics, I opened a new label, named Nicole, which moved from junior's wear to ladies wear. The line took off so much that I had to open yet *another* factory.

3. On the theory that the 78 million baby boomers were now having kids of their own, I went back into the children's business. We found a way to solve the problem of making our garments flame retardant in a cost-efficient way, and our new lines were a huge success. Actually, all we had done was to take the designs we had created for juniors and adapt them for children's wear, but that in itself was considered innovative at the time.

4. We went into direct mail-order sales, kicking things off by taking full-page ads in three of the biggest magazines in the fashion field. For the most part, we got a very modest return—perhaps twenty or thirty orders for most of the

items being offered for sale—with the exception of one garment, which was a kind of old-fashioned union suit with a drop-seat (we called it a "trap-door"); we got a couple of hundred responses to that one garment alone. But with only one of the garments selling well via direct mail-order, I couldn't justify the amount of time we'd need to spend on the project, so I pulled the plug. Of course, if I could have gazed into a crystal ball and foreseen the rise of online commerce, I would have stuck with it, but in those days there was barely a personal computer in sight, much less an Internet.

CHOICE EQUALS FREEDOM

Diversification not only saved Jennifer Dale, it also saved me personally on more than one occasion. In fact, I once lost a six-figure sum on a single investment. It hurt, to be sure, but what lessened the pain was the fact that I had *made* well over that from some of the other things I had put money into.

That's the beauty of diversification: when one investment tanks, another one works out. When one stock takes a nosedive, another one skyrockets. It's really just pure statistics: the odds of everything going down in value at the same time are low—just as low, in fact, as the odds of everything going up at the same time. No one's smart enough to pick only winners; some of your investments are bound to lose money. But if you anticipate those losses and offset them by making other investments in other areas that are unlikely to be affected at the same time, things will at least even out. Choose those investments wisely, and you will end up on the plus side of the balance sheet.

There's nothing new in what I'm saying, of course. Every financial adviser worth his salt and just about every financial self-help book ever written will tell you to diversify your investments, for just these reasons.

But I'm not just talking about buying Stock A and then buying Stock B. That's not diversification to me. I'm talking about putting your money into many different things, but *always in areas you have an interest in or some knowledge of.* That way, not only do you stack the odds in your favor, but you will get something positive out of even your losing investments.

I believe that choice equals freedom. There are thousands of different investments out there, thousands of places to put your money and I strongly urge you to spread your money around. Put it in many different baskets... but pick those baskets carefully. Stick with the things you know well, or the things that will at least give you pleasure.

But be careful, because there can be a downside to diversification as well.

WHEN ONE BASKET IS TOO MANY

Within months of Jennifer Dale's breakthrough success, I was being approached by all sorts of people with all sorts of investment schemes. Some of them were obviously shady but others appeared reputable, and as I considered those offers I had to keep reminding myself that it would be foolish to put too much money into any one idea, no matter how tempting it looked.

A case in point was one fellow who was trying to get me to invest our entire pension plan in real estate in Chicago and New Orleans. On the face of it, it sounded plausible—after all, how could you lose in real estate? (This was before my own disastrous personal investment in New York City real estate tax shelters.) But there was a little voice inside me that said that this fellow was pushing a little too hard to get me to put all my pension money in his one basket, and so I had my brother Sam, who was an architect, get on a plane and check the properties out firsthand. Sam took one look and advised me not to touch the investment because he felt the real estate in question was overpriced.

Six months later I found out that the fellow pushing this investment on me was in jail for fraud.

I'm not saying that I would have been dumb enough to have turned over our company's pension to this guy without checking his credentials, but what I am saying is that it was his insistence that I invest *all* of our pension funds with him—in other words, to ignore all my common sense instincts about diversification— that served as a major red flag and caused me to investigate in depth, thus saving Jennifer Dale's retired employees from potential financial disaster.

So there's an important corollary to the rule that says, "If it seems too good to be true, it probably *is* too good to be true," and that is, "If someone is trying to get you to invest *all* your money with them, it's probably not worth investing *any* of your money with them." I can't stress this more strongly: Diversification, in areas that you know, understand, have an interest in, or can exert some degree of control over, is the path to follow. Not only is it the best way to keep your overall net worth growing steadily if not spectacularly, it can sometimes be all that stands between you and disaster.

"Diversify or die" was a popular saying in the turbulent 1980s and 1990s, when it was all an individual or company could do to keep up. Today, I would modify that to, "Diversify and survive." Whichever spin you put on it, it's the only smart way to invest.

CHAPTER NINE

DON'T MAKE A MOVE WITHOUT A MAVEN

"Quality will long be remembered when price is forgotten"
—*Sir Henry Royce, co-founder of Rolls-Royce*

IN 1976, I TURNED 50, and I realized that I had to reinvigorate the design aspect of Jennifer Dale; I needed a larger vision of where styling was going to go. The way to do it, I thought, was to expose our designers to the world of fashion outside the United States. So I sent one of my top designers to Europe for ten days, where she visited stores in England, Italy, and France. She brought back lots of great ideas. One trend she had observed is what has since become the big fashion in women's underwear: camisoles and non-restricting bras—all the things that Jockey and Hanes now make, but designer quality. However, much as I liked the samples she brought back, I didn't think that was our business.

Big mistake. I should have moved Jennifer Dale into that area, because in retrospect I'm convinced that we would have done extremely well.

But somehow she wasn't able to talk us into it at the time, and it began to dawn on me that it made sense for me to accompany my designers on those trips because if we saw something over there that we felt was a winning design, I was the one person who could come back and immediately implement it. After all, as the company owner, no one was really going to argue with me if I felt something was a particularly good (or bad) idea; certainly they couldn't override me. There's that old expression: we're all equal... but I'm a little more equal.

For the next twenty years, I made at least four trips a year to Europe, totalling over a hundred trips overseas. I'd bring Estelle with me, along with a coterie of my designers, and we'd go around to all the boutiques and big stores searching for trends and new ideas. On one particular trip, everywhere I went, all I saw were jumpsuits. When I got back, I called the merchandise man at Sears and I told him, "You have a ski pajama of ours in your Christmas catalog. I want you to take it out and substitute a new jumpsuit I'm making." This was mid-July, but their holiday catalog had already gone off to the printer. He explained that it might cost twenty-five or thirty thousand dollars to make a substitution that late in the season. He thought I was crazy, but I insisted he do it.

I was taking a gamble, but I trusted my instincts. After all, I'd seen those jumpsuits in all the stores all over Europe, so I was pretty confident that they would be a big seller here too. It turned out I was right. That season, Sears sold over a hundred thousand of those jumpsuits. Years later, this fellow presented me with an award, inscribed with a paraphrasing of the Dean Witter line. It said, "When Marvin Tolkin talks, everybody listens."

Without realizing it, I had become a maven.

MAVENS IN MY LIFE

"Maven" is a word which basically describes someone who is especially proficient, but like so many words that have their origins in Yiddish, it actually has a more nuanced meaning. I especially like Princeton University's WordNet definition of a maven: "Someone who is dazzlingly skilled in any field." In other words, an expert's expert.

If you can find one of these people in the field you want to invest in, you have struck gold.

If you think about it, you've probably known many mavens in your life. I know I have, and all of them had a big impact on me and helped shape my destiny. My father, who provided me with so many important lessons in life as well as in business, was the first of them. Then there was a man named Bernie Davis, who had been an assistant secretary in the Department of Labor, under FDR. I was a young man, fresh out of college, when I began to work for my father. He knew that I needed seasoning, so he brought in Mr. Davis as a kind of outside consultant, with the assignment of teaching me how to handle personnel. Bernie spent three years coaching me, coming into the office one or two days a week. He'd attend executive meetings with me where company problems were being discussed, and afterwards he'd sit down with me and critique me, tell me what I had done well, what I hadn't, what I should have done, what I shouldn't do.

The crucial thing I learned from Bernie Davis was this: If there's a problem, don't rely on the story filtered through other people's perspectives: instead, get off your butt and find out for yourself. ("Go and see!" was the exact phrase he used.) Every time I followed his advice, it saved me money, time and heartache because I was able to cut through the baloney. I was right there with the operator who couldn't make her quota, the cutter who had a problem with piece goods, the machine that didn't work.

Mr. Davis gave me a firsthand illustration of a problem he had faced during World War II. There was one particular production plant in Ohio where productivity was starting to decline because everybody was complaining about the temperature in the factory: one employee was too hot, while another one was too cold. Bernie visited the plant and talked with the workers before coming up with a solution. He ordered thermostats to be installed all around the plant, one on every pole, and he told the workers that they could adjust them as they liked. Of course, the thermostat wires went up into the ceiling... and then went nowhere. It may have been a little sneaky, but the problem disappeared because the workers felt it had been dealt with. They played around with the thermostats all day long and they were happy. Even though the temperature didn't change by a single degree, everybody felt better because they felt in control. That's the power of the human mind—if you believe something is happening, then it's happening: perception is reality.

In the course of my retirement planning, the perfect example of a maven was the manager at the London store who advised me on buying Faberge pieces for more than two decades. I can state with a great degree of certainty that he knew more about that field than probably anybody, with the exception of Carl Faberge himself. The proof lies in the substantial profits I made when I began selling off the pieces, and in the fact that even his own store bought back many of them at several times the price I paid!

In fact, if you look at my retirement plan—certainly if you look at the aspects that were successful—you can identify a maven for every component. My son Larry was my maven in the stamp business. Jayne was my maven in the Michigan apparel business, and Les my maven in the swimsuit business. Ditto for Louis, the coin store proprietor who advised me to buy the Chinese Panda instead of South African Krugerrands.

In terms of those components related to Jennifer Dale, I largely served as my own maven, although I had the benefit of expert advice from many other smart individuals. One of these was the first attorney we had, a fellow named Leon Jaffe, who was a real expert in corporate law. He taught me that you can do a lot of things with just a little bit of money... if you're smart. At one point in the throes of our company's expansion, we bought a factory in midtown Manhattan. We needed a factory urgently, and this one appeared to meet all our needs so we bought it almost on the spur of the moment. The price was twelve or thirteen thousand dollars (a lot of cash for the time), and Leon had very little time to prepare the paperwork, but when we went to the closing he had worked things out so that the factory was a complete tax writeoff and cost us exactly nothing. The guy who was selling it couldn't believe the deal—he got his money in full but we didn't spend anything.

My partners in Jennifer Dale were also mavens. One of them had worked as an apprentice for my father and so he was in charge of cutting and pattern making for us. He was intellectually curious, and he wanted to learn about every facet of the business, so we sent him to school at night and he got even smarter and better. When computers first began appearing, he recognized their value to our industry in terms of maximizing cloth usage and he was determined to learn how to use them; eventually he taught all our other patternmakers how to use them too. Everybody else at the time went out and hired a computer consultant to make their patterns, but he became so proficient at it we actually started making patterns for our competitors! It became a business unto itself: Jennifer Dale was making thousands of dollars every week doing the labor for other manufacturers.

All of my partners, in fact, knew everything they had to know. I trusted these guys implicitly and they trusted me. There was no competition: everything was cooperative. We learned together, we grew together, we shared all the information that we had, and we worked everything out among us.

As I described in the last chapter, my brother Sam also once acted as my maven, when he checked out this shady character who was trying to get me to invest my company's pension in real estate. That's the way I did things. If I wasn't sure, I found someone who knew the lay of the land and I hired them to check it out for me.

Of course, there's no point to having a maven if you're not willing to listen to him or her. You have to have faith in their judgement, and you have to accept that they know more than you in their particular area of expertise. Sadly, I've found that a lot of people are afraid to surround themselves with smart people, because of the intimidation factor: they're afraid that the smart people may be smarter than *they* are. But in fact the reverse is true: If you surround yourself with smart people, they teach *you* all the time. You can't possibly put a value on how people like that can add to the richness of your life.

The one time I disregarded that rule, I lost big-time. I'm referring, of course, to my oft-lamented investment in real estate tax shelters. That was a terrible decision, and Sol Bergstein, our long-time business accountant—the same man who told my father that he had to either treat me as his partner or his son—warned me not to do it. Sol was tough, but straight... and very, very smart. He told me I was crazy to even consider such an investment because he knew that I didn't understand what I was getting into. He knew even less about the investment than I did, but something about it felt all wrong to him... and he was absolutely correct. If I'd put my money into bonds instead, as Sol advised, I would have done much better. Sure, today, those same buildings are worth ten times what we paid for them... but in the interim I nearly got wiped out.

FINDING THE RIGHT MAVEN

The most important thing about a maven is knowledge. The second most important thing is what he or she does with that knowledge; in other words, can you trust them to use their knowledge for your benefit? There are people who have a great deal of information at their fingertips, but at their core they are salespeople; their intention is to use their knowledge only for their own benefit. It's much harder to find a maven who is willing to help *others*, someone who truly is looking out for your best interests first and foremost. (By the way, the smartest mavens know that helping others and creating long-term relationships is a win/win situation because it's the best way to build a reputation... and ultimately the best way to help themselves too.)

When it comes to identifying an expert—especially someone who will advise you on something as important as accumulating money for your retirement—there is absolutely no substitute for word of mouth. Here's where it is vital to tap into your network, your circle of personal friends and business acquaintances. Ask around. Talk to everyone you know. Find out who's given them good advice—on any subject—and who's given them bad advice. Follow up. Contact the people they recommend (obviously, stay away from the ones they *don't* recommend!) and ask lots of questions. Get a feel for who they are, and get referrals: this is especially important if you're thinking of investing in a business venture with them. You need to be proactive in finding your maven; you can't just sit around and wait for the perfect expert to simply enter your life at random.

If you absolutely can't get a direct recommendation from someone you know, the second best thing is to look at that person's track record... although it can be difficult to determine the veracity of that record; after all, anyone who gives you a track record is only going to give you the record they want you to see! Sometimes the only way to find out someone's true motivation is to do a sample: based on their advice, buy a small item instead of a large one, or make a modest investment instead of a significant one and see how it works out.

You need to be open to new ideas and new people, and you need to abandon all preconceived notions, whether they are of the "this guy is the perfect guy for me" brand or whether they are the, "there's nothing this guy can do to help me" variety. Of course, the more homework you do, the better, but at the end of the day you simply have to trust your instincts. Nowhere is this more important than when it comes to finding the right professional— the right lawyer, accountant, or doctor. This is something you cannot be passive about. After all, as one of the finest physicians I ever knew once told me, the difference between a good doctor and a great doctor can be the difference between life and death.

ACTING AS YOUR OWN MAVEN

Sometimes you need to accept that no one knows more about a particular area than you yourself do. In those cases, you need to trust your own judgment and act as your own maven. I did that when it came to buying art and artifacts, where I simply bought things that I liked.

However, I was looking to make money from these objects as well—I viewed them as an investment opportunity for my retirement, not just as things I could have around me and enjoy. So I didn't just buy things blindly. Instead, I followed a few basic rules:

1. Wherever possible, I bought limited editions. The beauty of a limited edition is that there is only ever going to be a fixed, small quantity of that particular object made, thus increasing the potential demand.

2. I tended to buy name artists in preference to unknown ones, because those are the pieces that are more likely to appreciate in value.

3. I followed the advice of the old shopkeeper in Paris (the gentleman who originally steered me towards buying Faberge) when it came to making purchases of art and artifacts. He taught me to buy one item at the highest amount I could afford, as opposed to several things that add up to that amount. In other words, if you have a hundred dollars to spend, don't buy a hundred items for a dollar apiece; instead, buy one hundred-dollar item, because more expensive items stand a greater chance of appreciating in value.

4. I know that everybody's always looking for a bargain, but I often reflect on the old saying, "Quality will long be remembered when price is forgotten." That means

that you shouldn't invest in any object that isn't the best quality you can find in your price range. Of course, that doesn't work a hundred percent of the time. I once bought a diamond that was of such high quality that it had a limited amount of people who were interested in it. It was flawless, the right color, everything... which made it unaffordable for most people. That's equivalent to buying stock in a small company that trades in low volumes—if there's a limited demand, it almost doesn't matter what it's worth because you can't sell it. So always reach for quality more than price.

5. I always bought at places where there was a maven who could at least steer me in the right direction. They may have shown me ten objects, out of which I picked the four I liked... but I had confidence that all ten would have appreciated—just some more than others.

For fifty years, I sold underwear. As a professional salesman, of course I steered my customers in particular directions, but I can also honestly say that I never knowingly sold garments that I thought were wrong for a store. Integrity was the cornerstone of all my dealings. It was vital that people trusted me, and they did because they knew I was honest. That's how I stayed in business for so long.

It's not always possible to mix honesty and diplomacy, though. Believe me, I've told many people things that they didn't want to hear, things that could be hurtful. But I've always told them those things on the basis of being helpful and constructive, and I've never backed away from doing so. From the very first day that I started working for my father, I always worked from one principle, and that principle was: whatever I do, I've got to give you the best that's in me.

Take, for example, that great opportunity I had with Sears, when I was asked to put together that huge order. I was not only putting my expertise on the line, I was putting my entire company on the line. But the buyer knew that I believed in what I did and that I was honestly telling her what I thought was best for her stores, that I was steering her to the items that I felt would easily sell and make a good profit for her. And even if I got it disastrously wrong, I knew I had given it my best shot, and that I had been completely upfront. Again, you have to be prepared to make those kinds of decisions. You can't be afraid, even though you might fail.

As we have seen, nobody's smart enough to avoid making mistakes. Add to that the observation that nobody's smart enough to know everything about everything, and you'll understand the importance of never making a move—or at least never making a significant investment—without a maven.

CHAPTER TEN

MAKING THE REST OF YOUR LIFE THE BEST OF YOUR LIFE

"Life begets life. Energy becomes energy. It is by spending
oneself that one becomes rich."
—*Sarah Bernhardt*

AFTER NEARLY THREE DECADES of hard work and perserverance,
Jennifer Dale had established itself as the leader in its
field. We had a spotless reputation and we were selling into
the classiest stores in the country. The orders were pouring in
and our garments were moving out the door as fast as we could
make them. To keep up with the demand, we opened plants
in the Phillipines and eventually even in China. I was on top of
the world.

Then, in the blink of an eye, my world came crashing down.

Estelle had never been a complainer, so when she began
experiencing some medical problems in the fall of 1993, I took
it seriously... even if she didn't. I tried my best to persuade her
to get some tests done in the hospital, but she was focused on
preparing for the Jewish holidays, which was always an important
time for us, a time when we could enjoy the company of all our
children and grandchildren.

Six months later, Estelle began suffering severe pains. It was obvious that she needed urgent medical attention, and I drove her straight to the hospital. But it was too late. She soon lapsed into a coma, and less than a week later, she was gone.

I was devastated; I felt as if I had lost everything. Sure, I still had my family and friends, but the one person that I relied on most—my confidante, my partner, the woman I loved—was no longer there for me.

It was the toughest thing I ever had to go through. Every day felt unreal, like I was walking in a dream state. I was depressed, unfocused, unable to see any real meaning in life. Estelle and I had so many plans for the future, and now those dreams were shattered. The idea that I wouldn't be growing old with her after all was incomprehensible to me; I had spent nearly half a century vested in that belief, certain that it would happen.

In the midst of all this grief, there was confusion too. I started getting calls from friends offering to set me up with different single women they knew. They were well-meaning, but it was the last thing I was looking for. I was 68 and I had been happily married for 45 years. Frankly, the thought of dating terrified me! Dazed and overwhelmed, I decided to go to Europe for a few weeks to clear my head.

During that time away, I reflected on my life, and upon my marriage. I also reflected on something Estelle had said to me many years before. "If anything ever happens to me," she told me in her no-nonsense way, "I want you to find someone else. I want you to get married again." I brushed aside the idea at the time—I couldn't imagine living my life without her—but she knew that I was someone who needed the closeness of a companion, that I wouldn't do well on my own.

Still, I had no desire to reenter the dating scene, so it was with great trepidation that I returned home to try to put together the rest of my life. For the first few months, I immersed myself in work. But eventually I realized that in order to be a whole person, I had to open my heart to the possibility of a loving relationship once again. Without knowing it, I had already met the person who would make that possible. Remarkably, the catalyst for that meeting was Estelle's father (who also happened to be one of *my* father's closest friends), Bob Judelson.

As I've mentioned, Bob was a successful businessman who ran his own auto parts distribution company. He was also an eternal optimist who had the constitution of an ox, so he had worked well into his 90s and only retired reluctantly. Fortunately, he enjoyed relatively good health until shortly before he passed away at the tender age of 96, two years before Estelle died. Even in his retirement years, Bob remained alert and full of life, and so we had urged him to begin attending the local senior citizen center on a regular basis. One day I drove him there and as I walked him inside, he introduced me to their executive director. Her name was Carole and she was a gerontologist who was very active in various senior advocacy organizations. Not long after, Carole called and invited me to become a member of their board of directors. I was enormously impressed with her enthusiasm and compassion, and I felt I could help, so I agreed.

When I got back from Europe following Estelle's passing, a fellow board member got in touch and urged me to get together with Carole socially. (I found out some time later that he had been equally lobbying Carole!) We began having lunch on a regular basis and soon discovered that we had many things in common, not least of which was a thirst for knowledge and a strong sense of family. As we explored our commonalities, our friendship began deepening, then, over time, developed into a romance.

In 1996, Carole and I wed, and we have been enjoying a happy life together ever since. Incredibly, the same man—Bob Judelson—was responsible for introducing me to both of the women I was to fall in love with and marry. I take that as a sign that destiny was at play: I was destined to meet Carole and have a wonderful second life. I have no idea why I should be so blessed. I consider myself among the luckiest people to walk this earth.

A few months before our wedding, I made the decision to retire and turn Jennifer Dale over to my two youngest sons. As my father had done with me decades earlier, I felt I had taught them everything I knew, and I hoped that they would be able to carry the torch. Unfortunately, though, after a few years of struggle, they were forced to close the company down. The business aspect of my life was over, and a new chapter was about to begin.

But I have no regrets, and I learned so much throughout my working years, both in terms of business and personal relationships. The key to the success of Jennifer Dale was innovation, but we never could have achieved that success without our many talented employees. Everyone made a contribution, from the highest-powered executive to the part-time sewing machine operator. I've tried never to forget that in my dealings with people: everyone is important.

For the first six or seven months of my retirement I didn't know what to do with myself, but I was determined not to sit at home and fade away. I began doing some charity work but soon realized that the politics at play, both internal and external, can be a real headache. I started taking courses at various schools because I had an interest in both expanding and sharing my knowledge, but I had no clear direction in mind. I sought advice from everyone I knew—lawyers, accountants, clergymen—and I tested the waters with several different activities, but the more I tested, the more I realized, that's not me.

The problem was that I was trying to reinvent the wheel.

The answer, when it came, was clear as day. I had built a company around chasing demographics. I had followed the baby boomers as they got older and older, and that approach had brought me great success in the business world. With those baby boomers now on the verge of becoming seniors, wouldn't it make sense in my retirement years to continue to follow them and work for their best interests?

Especially given Carole's extensive experience and contacts in the field, it was an idea that fit me like a glove. She soon put me in touch with many of the leaders in the forefront of senior advocacy—people like geriatrician and Pulitzer Prize-winning author Dr. Robert N. Butler (then the head of Mount Sinai's geriatric department and today the CEO of the International Longevity Center); author David Wolfe (whose groundbreaking book, "Ageless Marketing," is a must-have for anyone seeking insight into the baby boomer generation); and Igal Jellinek, executive director of the Council of Senior Centers and Services (CSCS), an organization which serves 300,000 senior citizens every day in the city of New York.

Ever since then, I have been involved fulltime in advocating for seniors through my service on the boards of various organizations, and through my work as a business consultant for CSCS. I've also started mentoring a number of individuals who are building new post-retirement careers, and I have even embarked on a round of public speaking engagements on the subject of retirement planning. Carole and I travel all around the country—indeed, all over the world—attending conferences and exchanging ideas with the leading experts in the field, doing all we can to try to improve the lives of our aging population. It's been the most fulfilling thing I have ever done.

Retirement, I have learned, is best approached as a gradual transition to a new life, not the termination of an old one. View it as you would a career change with exciting new challenges. Anticipate it with eagerness, not dread. Certainly retirement is not the end of productivity. After all, Benjamin Franklin invented the bifocal at the age of 78; Giuseppe Verdi composed "Ave Maria" when he was 85; Frank Lloyd Wright was working on the design of the Guggenheim Museum at 91. We may not all be a Franklin, a Verdi, or a Wright, but I firmly believe we *all* have the capacity to change the world, even if only an inch at a time.

THE IMPORTANCE OF PURPOSE

My father was 62 when he turned over his business to me, and he lived to be 79. He had always been a highly motivated individual, and during his later years, he basically did five things: he learned how to play the piano, he learned how to paint, he became religious, he attended all the classes he could at the New School, and he became a member of the Institute of Retired Professionals. For more than a decade, he split his time between New York and Florida.

But as I observed my father's retirement, it became sadly obvious that only a certain amount of enthusiasm and motivation can last for only a certain number of years, because if you don't reach out and do something purposeful, it's very difficult to keep regenerating that interest. When he became ill at 74, he really was spent—his vitality was gone and he was really just existing, not living. Ever since then I have been determined not to let history repeat itself.

I spent my entire career serving customers, serving employees, serving suppliers, serving banks, serving the union, serving dozens of different constituencies. I had to do it because that's the nature of running a successful business—you have to try to satisfy everyone. When I retired, I decided it was time to satisfy *me*, first and foremost... and that meant not doing anything I didn't have a passion for. Whatever it is you choose to do, you should do it only because you *want* to, not because somebody is expecting it of you. More than just giving you a reason to wake up every day, that's what will create a vibrancy in the last third of your life, a *joie de vivre*. For many people, retirement starts with a brief period of exhilaration and liberation, followed by a long and steep decline as they cast about for meaning. Unfortunately, if you don't replace work with something engaging and important to you, you could be in for a long, sad haul—or a short, sad haul.

So retirement should be viewed as something a lot more than just an extended vacation: *you have to have purpose.*

The importance of purpose cannot be overstated; in fact, the very key to life is purpose. According to biologists, human beings once had tails—the coccyx. They didn't need the tail, so it disappeared. It's the same with purpose: if you have no purpose, you disappear.

Understanding the importance of purpose requires no leap of faith—it's scientific fact. As David Wolfe has said, "Purpose is the animating force of life." He goes on to explain:

"Animals in the wild that no longer have purpose often are forsaken by their own or taken out by predators...One of the most remarkable illustrations of the irreplaceable role of purpose in our lives is the cellular process of apoptosis—what biologists often refer to as cell suicide. When a cell in your body ceases to have a purpose it literally ends its own life."

There's proof positive: *purpose actually sustains life... and, conversely, lack of purpose is literally suicide.* Good health and longevity, of course, go hand in hand, and there's a lot of research that indicates that retirees who remain engaged by volunteering, learning, or working (albeit at a more relaxed, flexible pace) maintain better health: not just physical health, but mental and emotional health as well. Studies conducted at the National Institutes of Health, for example, have shown an association between life expectancy and individuals who had goals and a sense of purpose in life.

To have a full life, three things are essential: *involvement, purpose,* and *passion.* If you don't really care about something, you're never going to succeed in it... and the same is true of your retirement. Having your health is one thing—an extremely important thing, to be sure—but there's also a richness to life that has to be explored and tested all the time. It's not something you can lose and hope to get back, either. Once you drop out, once you get separated from the active part of life, it's extremely difficult to jump back in. Life is something that has to be continually experienced.

Everybody wants to have it all. Unfortunately, too many people think that "all" simply means money. They're wrong. All that is good in life comes from involvement... even if that involves heartache too.

The Need To Be Needed

In any endeavor, socialization is a key component to success. You can't reach the top of your profession without being able to interact and work well with others, without the ability to not only be a team leader, but a team player at times.

The same is true when it comes to making the most of your retirement years. In fact, there have been dozens of studies that show that socialization is essential to both health and longevity. A recent study conducted by the University of Pennsylvania Institute concluded that the more engaged you are with other people, the more healthy you are likely to be... and, of course, the healthier you are, the longer you're likely to live.

Having solid relationships with other people—your husband or wife, your boyfriend or girlfriend, your brother, your sister, close friends—is a big part of living a long and happy life. I've been involved with the Meals On Wheels program for some years now. Care to guess what the most important part of the program is? That's right: socialization. When a driver delivers a meal, he spends five or ten minutes chatting with the person he's delivering the food to... and it turns out that that's more important than the meal itself.

Networking is a vital part of the business world, to be sure, but it's just as essential in your personal life. The more friends and colleagues you have, the more opportunities you have to ask questions of people who have experience and/or expertise in areas that you have little or no familiarity with. Getting their perspective is what helps you to make better decisions.

You will find that your friends and family become even more important to you after you stop working, so do what you can to shore up and strengthen your existing relationships... at least the ones you feel really good about.

But you also need to be realistic, and accept that at least some of the relationships you had prior to retirement—especially professional relationships formed in the workplace—will not remain nearly as strong as they had been in the past. Instead, you have to go out and actively seek new relationships. Think about where you might meet people who have similar interests to you: clubs, trade shows, social functions, your place of worship. Then go there and be proactive. Stick out your hand and introduce yourself. You might be pleasantly surprised at the positive responses you receive. After all, there are probably a lot of people there for the same reason you are: to meet new people.

And as you meet new people, think of them as guides helping you cross a river. Everybody has something to teach. You just have to be able to recognize what they have to offer.

I think Dr. Sherwin Nuland of the Yale University School of Medicine put it best when he said, "To age well is to always keep moving forward emotionally and reaching out for mutual caring and connectedness with other people. Ultimately, meaningful relationships are the answer to everything in old age."

Clearly, socialization is one of the keys to living a long and happy life. But even more important is *being needed*. That's something I learned from observing my father's last years. For all his energy and motivation, for all the various activities he undertook, he still felt dissatisfied; there was an emptiness within him which neither he nor I could identify at the time. With the benefit of hindsight, I now know the cause: it was because most of the things he was doing were within himself.

This was a man who had spent half a century being in the center of things—people were always asking his advice, soliciting his opinion, turning to him for guidance in big decisions and small, professional and personal. But after he retired, those calls stopped coming. For all he was doing to improve himself inwardly, he must have felt—at least on an unconscious level—that he no longer was needed. In my opinion, that's a big reason why his post-retirement years were so short and unfulfilling.

The need for recognition is universal. It's instilled in all of us to some degree or other, and you can't just turn it off when your working days are behind you. Recognition is vital for buttressing up your sense of self-worth, building your self-confidence. In your retirement years, you may well have to search out activities that satisfy that need. When I serve on boards and I get thanked for my time or input, I always respond by saying that they are doing as much for me as I do for them, and that is the absolute truth. They feel they need me, and that in turn makes me feel needed. I want to stay valuable. I want to feel good about myself. And I don't think I'm different from anyone else.

The longer I live, the more I realize that having purpose and being needed is so important that it can actually override other aspects of life... even poor health. The people I know who are happiest all have a purpose—or even several purposes—to their lives... even if they are suffering from ill-health.

So take your passion and go in as many different directions as you can with it. Being able to carry on conversations about many different topics, and being fairly knowledgeable about them, will make people *want* to talk to you. This is the way to hold on to friends and to make new friendships. Everybody wants that kind of interaction; they want to be able to speak with someone who knows what they're talking about. And that's good for longevity, because people will want to be with you. They'll need you.

WHY STOP WORKING?

It used to be that the terms "working" and "retirement" were mutually exclusive: you worked for as long as you could (or for as long as you chose to work), and then, when you stopped, you were considered retired. But, as we've seen, starting with the baby boomer generation, everything has changed. Today it's become commonplace to continue working well into your retirement years; in fact, Merrill Lynch reports that 71 percent of American adults intend to keep working in retirement, with most expecting to retire from their current job or career at around 61 and then launch into an entirely new career. A 2003 AARP survey showed that 79 percent of baby boomers plan to *never* stop working.

Clearly, the entire concept of retirement is changing. In 2002, the World Health Organization issued a report stating that "it is time for a new paradigm, one that views older people as active participants in an age-integrated society and as active contributors... [the paradigm should challenge] the traditional view that learning is the business of children and youth, work is the business of midlife, and retirement is the business of old age." Future attitudes toward retirement are likely to move sharply away from the simplistic view of all work before retirement and no work after.

Larry Cohen, Vice President of SRI Consulting Business Intelligence, has in fact suggested that people rethink retirement as occurring in not one, but four stages:

1. Preretirement, when you attempt to accumulate assets specifically for the time you stop working.

2. Something he calls "revolving retirement," when you perhaps try a new field or two for awhile, take a short-term

position, or otherwise move in and out of the workforce to keep busy and/or delay drawing on benefits like Social Security and pensions.

3. Middle retirement, a lukewarm version of revolving retirement, when you're partly living off your benefits and investments, supplemented by a nominal income derived from part-time work.

4. Late retirement, or what we once knew simply as "retirement," when you stop working completely and are completely dependent on your benefits and investments.

There are many, many excellent reasons to continue working after retirement. There's the extra income, of course, not to mention continued healthcare benefits. Then there are all the other financial benefits that come from continuing to work, as we discussed in Chapter One: more opportunity to contribute to Social Security and your 401(k) and company pension plan, more time to accumulate interest on your assets, and reducing the time those assets must support you. Each year you delay claiming Social Security, your monthly benefits increase by 7 - 8 percent. Delay it by two years and your monthly check goes up 15 percent; delay it by four years and your check will actually be one-third higher than it would have been if you began drawing benefits at the minimum age.

There are plenty of intangible benefits too: the positive socialization aspects of continuing to interact with others in the workplace, and the self-satisfaction you get from being needed and from performing a job that you enjoy. One prominent study published in 2005 concluded that the most satisfied retirees were those who participated in multiple productive activities, including volunteering as well as paid work. Such engagement not only helps people adjust to retirement but also improves their emotional and physical health. There's even clinical proof that mental stimulation improves cognitive function—that is, your ability to think—and reduces the kind of cognitive decline that accompanies illnesses like Alzheimer's. In fact, the Alzheimer's Association has identified four major components to staying healthy later in life: social connectedness, regular physical activity, mental stimulation, and a healthful diet. Working at something fulfilling or staying otherwise engaged is a good way to make the first three happen, especially if your job gets you off the couch, talking to people and learning new things.

For years, conventional science believed that you were born with a certain amount of neurons (that is, the cells that transmit electrochemical signals) in your brain and that, one by one, they died off as you got older... but, unlike the other cells in your body, they didn't replicate. Later research proved that they were wrong: neurons *do* replicate, new ones *do* grow, and it turns out that the most important factor in growing new brain cells is challenging your mind. Stimulating your brain—by continually presenting it with problems to solve and decisions to make—can literally help it to sprout new neurons. It turns out that with your brain, as with your muscles, you've got to use it or lose it. What better way to exercise your mind than to keep working?

What's more, the human brain can actually establish new pathways as old ones degenerate, or to compensate for neurological problems following disease or an accident. According to Dr. Nuland, "The brain is the only organ that determines how it ages. The more you stimulate it [by] engaging in mental activities that absorb you, the more *plasticity* you develop, increasing the number of synaptic connections between cells." In other words, you can actually slow down the aging process in your brain by thinking more!

To me, the formula is a simple one:

$$Keeping\ busy = Keeping\ well$$

So the busier you are in your retirement years, the better the chance you have of living not just a longer life, but a *healthier* one. I'm living proof of that! So was my father-in-law, who was still working at 90—perhaps not at the same level as when he was a younger man, but he was still going into the office every day, giving it his all.

I understand that, for most people, the whole point of working is to reach an end goal, to get to that day when they can finally take it easy and enjoy life. Unfortunately, it doesn't work that way: the fountain of youth actually springs from purposeful involvement. What you choose to do may look like work to an outsider, but if it's bringing you pleasure and fulfillment, if it's something you have a passion for, it can literally add years to your life.

And after all, as we've asked repeatedly in this book, what are you going to do with the last third of your life? Even if you love playing golf or tennis or bridge, even if you love traveling, even if you love reading and absorbing knowledge, you're going to get sick of it after awhile. The happiest retirees I've met are the people who not only do the things they love but also continue to work productively.

On the other hand, if all you do after you retire is take advantage of the early bird special at the local IHOP and stare at your television set, you might as well just lay down and wait to die. To keep living—not just living, but living a meaningful life—you've got to constantly challenge yourself, you've got to keep going out there and beat the bushes.

Life is a known quantity, so make the most of it. After all, none of us knows what's on the other side of the curtain.

GIVE OF YOURSELF

In his landmark work *Childhood and Society*, famed American psychologist and Pulizer Prize winner Erik Erikson wrote, "I am what survives of me." The older you get, the more you realize it's not about how much you accumulated while you were here on earth, but how much you *contributed*.

Retirement provides a fabulous opportunity to give of yourself. Once you stop working, or scale back on the number of hours you work, suddenly you have all this free time that you never had before. And, if you've done adequate planning, you will also have the financial freedom to pursue whatever activities you choose.

I found something I loved—advocating for the aging population—and it has provided me with an enormous amount of satisfaction in my retirement years. Find something that suits *your* abilities and interests, and devote yourself to it; give it as much time and energy as you possibly can. It will pay you back in spades, I guarantee it.

Giving of yourself is so much more fulfilling than just continuing on in an endless incarnation of your mid-life work. If you don't need the money, consider doing volunteer work. If you love children, volunteer at a children's hospital or kindergarten. If you love business, become a mentor. If you love academics, become a tutor. If you love gardening, help with the planting at your local nature preserve or botanic garden. If you love sports, coach or umpire the kids at your nearest school. If you love reading, work at your library. Whatever it is you have a passion for, find a way to involve yourself in that passion and at the same time give back to others.

One huge bonus of volunteering is that you'll be able to pretty much make your own schedule, allowing you to do good work on your own timetable. If you're one of those people who absolutely need rigid schedules, just set up your *own* rigid schedule... but set it up in such a way that works best for you.

I believe that everything you manifest springs from both your thought processes and your actions—the way you live your life, how you grow within yourself, how willing you are to give of yourself. I believe this because I have found that people respond positively to positive energy. If you reach out and give with a full heart, if you give the best advice you can each and every time you are asked, it will come back to you a hundredfold, and you will receive rewards that you may not even realize at the time.

Just as my successes in investing came from following my interests, so too has my success in retirement come from staying involved. I feel positively rewarded for reaching out and doing as much as I can to help others. And that feeling radiates to other people—they feel it too. It's like a giant mirror: you send out positive energy and it comes back and warms *you* at the same time. Believe me, there's nothing better than feeling good about yourself.

Aging Gracefully

Everybody wants to live long, but no one wants to grow old.

David Wolfe hit the nail on the head when he wrote those words in his book *Ageless Marketing*. Adding to the dilemma, as

Dr. Sherwin Nuland points out, "we still tend to regard aging as a disease over which we have limited control and one that robs us of independence and satisfaction."

But you know something? Growing old isn't all that bad. In many ways, you are better able to appreciate life and the world around you, because you have greater context to put it in. Retirement presents a golden opportunity for exploration and reflection, valuable time to learn and grow. It also provides an opportunity to make up for all the mistakes you made when you were younger and not nearly so wise, all the time you wasted, all the wrong paths you followed, all the wrong-headed decisions you made. Jonathan Swift, the author of *Gulliver's Travels*, once wrote, "The latter part of a wise person's life is occupied with curing the follies, prejudices and false opinions they contracted earlier."

That's what experience and wisdom brings. As Dr. Nuland puts it, "Aging is an art... because no matter how old you get, you still have a surprisingly wide variety of choices to shape and create the kind of life you want." And, he adds, "it's not inevitable that seniors must get weaker each year. That kind of thinking actually contributes to one's decline because you don't take actions that can invigorate you." Nuland goes on to observe that "people who age well view limitations as the realistic circumstances of their life—not as a punishment or burden."

Certainly the longer you live, the longer you're *going* to live. Medical science is improving, food quality is improving, gerontological knowledge is improving, even ecological problems such as global warming will—hopefully—soon be improving. So everything will be making it conducive to living longer and more productively, and in good health, both physically and mentally. In fact, Dr. Nuland predicts that "advances in fighting osteoporosis, arthritis, heart disease and cancer will enable many of us to live to age 100 with fewer limitations." What's more, he says, "we'll only suffer a severe decline in our health shortly before our natural death."

There's actually an intriguing chicken-and-egg situation going on here: If you stay healthy and age successfully, you will have the physical and mental resources to enjoy retirement. In turn, mental stimulation and physical activity will *keep* you healthy and happy. The New York Times recently reported a study that showed that "maintaining physical fitness is likely to stave off cognitive decline, and maintaining cognitive fitness and activity can also help forestall physical decline. They are all intimately linked in the aging process and are influenced by activities in both spheres, because they are not really separate spheres." In other words, physical fitness and mental fitness are actually one and the same. I have absolutely found this to be true in my own life; I'm probably more physically active now than I was during most of my working years. Every morning at 6 AM, you'll find me at the local gym, waiting for them to open the doors, and I can feel the benefit in terms of extra energy and stamina.

But don't just take my word for it. Scientists have found definitive proof that even the aging body reacts strongly to a regime of structured physical activity. In fact, Dr. Nuland has observed that "if you take a person in his/her 80s and put him on a supervised strengthening program of resistance training and weights, you can double his strength in six weeks... Strength training improves coordination and greatly reduces the chances of a slip-and-fall, which is often the event that leads to losing one's independence."

Above all, *don't ever quit on yourself.* Dr. Nuland sums it up best when he says, "No matter what your position or financial situation, creativity and curiousity are the keys to vitality in old age." Staying engaged will keep you young. Perhaps not forever young—that's still a few years away—but much younger than your chronological age anyway.

When all else fails, remember this: Growing old is a hell of a lot better than the alternative.

AFTER YOU'RE GONE

What happens after you die? None of us knows, but there's one thing we can be certain about: life will go on. Sure, people will miss you and they will grieve for you, but when the funeral is over and the tears start to dry, life for the people you leave behind will continue.

You've worked hard all your life to accumulate assets, to scrimp and save and plan for your retirement. But as you get older and face your own mortality, you need to start thinking about what will happen to those assets after you're gone. And just as it's vital that you make your own decisions throughout the course of your life, it's equally vital that you make the decisions about what happens to your earthly goods after your death. Trust me, it's nothing to be afraid of. After all, nobody's getting out of this world alive.

Of course, the decision as to what and how much you leave to your friends, family, and favorite charities is an intensely personal one, different for every individual. I'm not going to try to steer you in any particular direction, but I do want to share with you my thoughts about living with the decisions you make.

The first rule would seem to be, be fair, but don't create problems. Treating everybody equally isn't always a good solution, because the truth of the matter is that everybody *isn't* equal, and you can't make them so in your will. That doesn't mean that you don't love all your children equally, but you can't treat them as if they were all cut out of a cookie cutter, either. Nobody likes being treated that way, and making your decision on that basis alone will undoubtedly be unfair to somebody.

A friend of mine once pointed out that people like me who have made successes of their business often wind up turning it over to their children and losing every cent they made. That didn't happen to me, but it is quite common, and it's happened to a lot of people I know. All these people obviously believed that the best way to invest their money was in their children, but it turned out they were wrong.

So you have to be especially clear-headed about this decision, and you have to let logic (your head) override your emotions (your heart). Otherwise, you are almost certain to end up being unfair to someone—unfair to your spouse, unfair to one or more of your children, or unfair to yourself—and your passing will create dissension at a time when families most need to come together. Think carefully before you act.

A FINAL THOUGHT

I know plenty of people who retire, move someplace warm, and then sit around doing nothing day after day after day. They exist, and not much else. They may still keep breathing for some time, but it's really as if they've already died—they just won't get buried for another twenty years.

That's not the way I want to go out. To me, the only way to live is to *really* live, to get into the swing of things and stay there. I like to think of life as a fast-moving stream. You can't necessarily control how rapidly the water flows or where it goes but you at least want to be able to steer the boat... and you need to at least keep your head above water at all times so you don't drown.

The good news is that, as you go further and further downstream—that is, as you get older and older—it gets easier to navigate. You may go faster, but it goes easier because you have a better idea of how to deal with things successfully. You have the experience to know that even if the water goes around bends and swerves to the right or to the left, you have the ability to stabilize the boat and not fall in.

This builds throughout the course of your life—you don't start off at fifteen or twenty-five and have these kinds of skills; no one does. But as you get older, you get wiser and you learn how to maintain control. And I don't care what stream you're on: there are always rocks in your path, there are always twists and turns. You can't miss every boulder, but it's from your failures that you gain strength. You learn how to navigate around those boulders and rocks, and the more you do it, the more strength you have to face the next one. And the stronger you get, the more you are able to roll with the punches. You learn that hitting a rock won't necessarily kill you. It may hurt you a little bit, it may dent you financially or may render you mentally or physically incapacitated, at least for a time... but you learn that it won't kill you, so you develop the ability to say, "So what?" and you continue onwards.

These are the lessons you learn as you go through the passage of time. As the old Australian folk saying goes, "The older the fiddle, the sweeter the tune."

Take it from me: it really is true.

I wish for each and every one of you health, happiness, longevity, and prosperity.

Most of all, may you *live* all the days of your life.

EPILOGUE

THE TIMES,
THEY ARE A-CHANGING

SHORTLY AFTER COMPLETING *When I'm 64*, two major world events occurred which will undoubtedly have a huge impact on everyone's retirement planning, and on their lives in general. I'm talking, of course, about the financial crisis that began unfolding in late 2008 and the election of Barack Obama as president of the United States.

The weakening of the U.S. economy which led to the financial crisis has been on the horizon for some time now. In neighborhood after neighborhood, people with limited financial resources were misled by unscrupulous lending institutions into buying homes well above their means. With subprime mortgages serving as the carrot on a stick, millions of Americans soon found themselves in over their heads. Worse yet, with the subsequent collapse of the housing market, they discovered that the value of the properties they had purchased had plummeted. People had no choice other than to default and lose their homes, which in turn led to instability in the banking industry and the collapse of many financial institutions, including some of the largest ones. In order to prevent even more disastrous consequences—such as the failure of the entire economy—the U.S. government was forced to intervene, providing hundreds of billions of dollars (all of which will have to be borrowed from foreign banks, to be paid back, with interest, by the American taxpayers and their children and grandchildren) in a controversial bailout.

Like a wildfire, our homegrown financial catastrophe spread to markets overseas, and what began as a national crisis became a global one. No one should have been surprised about that. You know the old adage about how, when the United States gets a cold, the rest of the world gets pneumonia? It's completely true—even more so these days, when all the economies of the world are so interdependent on one another.

Was all of this preventable? Probably. I believe in free markets as much as anyone, but it's become clear from these events that a certain amount of regulation is required—otherwise, the foxes are in charge of the chicken coop. Right now, the way our government is trying to deal with the economic crisis reminds me of the little Dutch boy trying to plug a leak in a dam—they plug a leak here, they plug a leak there... until they start running out of fingers and hands. There are holes popping up all over the place, and the truth of the matter is that no one knows exactly how things will turn out.

But, as I have stressed over and over again in the pages of this book, mistakes are inevitable—even mistakes of this magnitude. The important thing is to learn from them and then move forward. And I do feel optimistic for the future, especially given the results of the last election. Barack Obama is a smart individual, and he has surrounded himself with smart people. Certainly, the fact that he's assumed the reins of power makes me feel a lot better about the future of Social Security and Medicare. For the first time in many years, it seems as if our leaders will look at these problems objectively and search for a real solution.

These same events have made me more convinced than ever before that people need to go forward with their retirement planning full speed ahead, despite the ups and downs of the economy. In all this upheaval lies opportunity. This is the time to invest. This is the time to make money. All you have to do is to read the signposts... and have a little intestinal fortitude.

It has become clear, for example, that the Obama administration is going pursue things like universal health care and improvements to our nation's infrastructure (roads, bridges, etc.), as well as a transition to alternative energy, so those are certainly areas to explore in terms of investment opportunities.

Opportunity, as we have seen, sometimes comes when you least expect it. I recently discovered that several of the paintings I own—actually bought by my first wife Estelle, many years ago—have greatly increased in value, due to the unfortunate demise of the artist, which, as often happens, propelled him from obscurity to fame.

This helps underline the importance of diversification. If I had followed conventional wisdom and put most of my money in stocks and bonds, as some of my friends did, I'd be in serious trouble now. When the market nosedived, I took a bath, for sure, but at least I didn't lose everything. (Thank goodness the Bush plan to allow investment of Social Security benefits in the market was blocked, or there would be a lot more people suffering today—people who could least afford it.)

I understand that not everybody can afford to spend a lot of money on art or other collectibles, but the point is that, whatever your budget, if you invest only in quality items, not only will you very rarely lose, you actually have a very good chance at turning a profit, possibly even a huge one.

And even though it takes longer to sell a picture than a stock—something which you can normally get rid of immediately—I'm more convinced than ever before that the retirement plan I put together was the right way to go. The events of the past few months have reinforced my belief that you should only put a modest percentage of your money into the stock market, just to hedge your bet, if you will. But don't forget that the best way to hedge your bet is to bet at lots of different windows; don't just bet on horses—spread your money around and bet on everything. Of course, all of this involves risk, but if you don't take any risks, you won't get much reward. That's why I don't keep my money in banks.

So what should you do if you're already heavily invested in the stock market? A lot depends on how old you are. If you're at or close to retirement age, the problem is that you may not live long enough for it to come back, so the best course of action might be cutting your losses and investing your money elsewhere. On the other hand, if you're in your forties or fifties and you've got significant investments in the stock market, you might well consider sitting tight, because the odds of the market making a complete recovery before you reach retirement age are pretty good. You've just got to be prepared to weather the storm and try not to get too discouraged when you see the value of your stocks continue to evaporate, because things may get worse before they get better.

Frankly, I don't think anybody—not even the so-called financial "experts"—know where this is going, or when it will end. After the stock market crash of 1929, it took a good twelve years, and a world war, to get things all the way back. Hopefully the recovery this time around will be a lot shorter, but nobody knows for sure *what* will happen. I am confident, however, that eventually the ship will be righted.

The only thing that I can't see in my crystal ball is the length of time it's going to take to right the ship. I do know this, though: it will happen, if for no other reason than that there are so many industrious people in the world who are prepared to work hard and take less. All throughout recorded history, there have been trying times, times of crisis. Some are worse than others, but human beings are adaptable, and they always strive to do better. In today's global society, we are truly all one, and that's never happened before in the entire history of the planet. That's why I'm convinced that, in the end, the financial debacle that's occurred will actually strengthen every country in the world.

We Americans have an unusual resiliency. We're like a thick rope, with each strand representing a different constituent, and every strand intertwined. Those strands aren't just grounded here, either—they go back to the countries where our immigrants came from: Ireland, Italy, Germany, Poland, Russia, Mexico, China, Japan, Nigeria, Kenya. We're all knotted together, and that means we all rise together or we all fall together.

That's the true strength of this nation: not just the number of strands in our rope, but how closely intertwined they are. And when you have a rope with all those strands in it, it's much stronger than just a solid piece of string. That's the strength of diversity.

That's why I continue to be not just hopeful, but optimistic about the future.

— Marvin Tolkin
February 2009

APPENDIX

FACTS AND FIGURES

"Wisdom is the abstract of the past,
but beauty is the promise of the future"
— Oliver Wendell Holmes

S TATISTICS HAVE A FUNNY EFFECT on people. Sure, there are some individuals who get excited when confronted with a page full of numbers and graphs (these are people who tend to gravitate to jobs with the US Census Bureau, or as compilers of actuarial tables), but for most of us, they just make our eyes glaze over.

But statistics can be very important, especially when they are relevant to your own life. We'd all like to have a crystal ball in which we could foresee the future, and while we know that it's an unrealistic expectation, the fact of the matter is that statistics can help serve that function...albeit in a kind of fuzzy way. In this Appendix, we'll take a closer look at the facts and figures that support the underlying premises in this book, most notably my belief that planning is necessary in order to enjoy a comfortable, stress-free, and meaningful life after retirement.

You've Got A Lot Of Living To Do

Statistics show, for example, that the years after your 64th birthday will in all likelihood account for a full third of your life. In 1900, a 64-year old man could expect to live for just another seven years on average.[1] In 1960, he could expect to stick around for another ten years.[2] But the tremendous advances in medicine since then have caused those numbers to rise sharply. The average life expectancy of someone born in the year 1000 was 25. During the twentieth century, that rose from 47 to 77, and it continues to rise dramatically and steeply.[3] By the year 2000, our typical 64-year old man was looking at another sixteen years of life, and by the year 2030, he'll probably have at least another eighteen years[4]; life expectancies for women are even higher.[5]

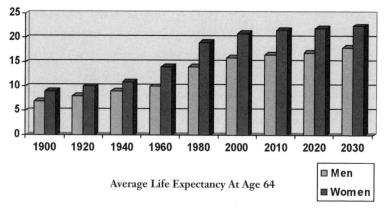

Average Life Expectancy At Age 64

☐ Men
■ Women

Of course, those are just average figures, which means that almost half the population can expect to stick around even longer. Soon living to 90 or even 100 will become commonplace; 20 percent of all women over the age of 64 today will live past 95.[6] Beginning in 2031, when the first baby boomers begin celebrating their 85th birthday, the number will increase rapidly. At that time, the

85-and-over population is expected to grow dramatically, reaching the staggering number of twenty-one million by the year 2050.[7]

This is really important stuff because it tells you that you've got a pretty good shot at having twenty, thirty, or possibly even forty years of life ahead of you after you retire. Perhaps even more importantly, with medical advances being what they are, you'll probably be able to enjoy most of those years in relatively good health. Not surprisingly, the health of those 64 and older has shown marked improvement over the past two decades. As shown in this graph,[8] the share of the elderly that lack the ability to function independently with ease has declined from 26.2 percent to 19.0 percent. What's more, even though dependency obviously rises sharply as people get older, there is nonetheless a clear pattern of decreasing dependency for *all* age groups.

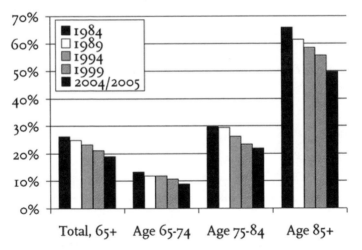

Percent of Older Americans with Any Kind of Disability, by Age, Selected Years 1984-2004/2005

So that's the good news: you'll probably be able to enjoy your retirement for many, many years. The question is, can you *afford* to retire?

Well, for one thing, you may not have any choice. A recent survey indicated that only 36 percent of current retirees retired when they planned to, while 7 percent retired later than expected. But a whopping 57 percent retired *earlier* than expected, mostly because of health reasons, job loss/downsizing, or the need to care for a spouse or family member.[9]

For some people, post-retirement expenses may be considerably lower than when they were working. Many homeowners (at least those not caught up in the sub-prime mortgage nightmare) will have fully paid the mortgage on their house, and the kids will probably be out of the nest and more or less self-sufficient. On the other hand, you can almost certainly expect to shell out a lot more for health care as you get older. The average retiree actually spends some $640 each month on health care[10], and even if the Medicare system remains at its current level of benefits (which it almost certainly won't), your out-of-pocket health costs will probably exceed $200,000 in the last decade of your life.[11]

So what *is* retirement, anyway? Good question. Let's take a closer look.

EVERYTHING YOU EVER WANTED TO KNOW ABOUT RETIREMENT (BUT WERE AFRAID TO ASK)

The idea of stopping work when you get older is something we take for granted today, but it's a concept that hasn't actually been in existence all that long. There was no such thing as retirement before 1889, when Germany became the first nation in the world to adopt an old-age social insurance program. In a ground-breaking letter to Parliament, Germany's Emperor, William the First, wrote: "...those who are disabled from work by age and invalidity have a well-grounded claim to care from the state."[12]

Before the early 20th century, when other nations (including the United States) began adopting similar programs, you simply worked until you were physically unable to do so, at which point either your children took care of you or you lived off your own wits until ending up in a pauper's grave. Families, of course, were larger then. This was due in part to the lack of birth control, but also because having more children increased the odds of someone being there to look after you in your old age.

One persistent myth about the German program is that it adopted 65 as the standard retirement age because that was the age of Chancellor Otto von Bismarck when the legislation was introduced. In fact, Bismarck was 74 at the time and Germany initially set the retirement age at 70; it was not until 27 years later (in 1916) that the age was lowered to 65.[13] Of course, in 1916 the average life expectancy in Germany was only 45 years,[14] so not too many people could reach the age where they could receive benefits... which may have been the whole point.

Pensions were also an invention of the 19th and 20th centuries. On the face of it, they were designed to provide more secure and more adequate income for non-working individuals. But, more ominously, they also provided an incentive for older workers (who have achieved relatively high salary levels through seniority) to leave employment so that the company could hire newer, younger workers (at a lower pay scale) to do the same job. (Sadly, this is something corporations continue to do with impunity, though today they substitute short-term severance packages for long-term pensions.) One almost accidental consequence of creating pensions was a dramatic decline in labor-force participation at later ages and the introduction of a new phase of life known as "retirement."

When President Franklin D. Roosevelt signed the Social

Security Act into law on August 14, 1935, average U.S. life expectancy was only around 62,[15] so 65 still seemed "old" to planners. What's more, at the time, there were only about 7 million Americans old enough to take advantage of the program. (Today, there are approximately 40 million people age 65 or older; by the year 2030, that number will nearly double.)[16]

Number of Persons 65+,
1900 - 2030 (numbers in millions)

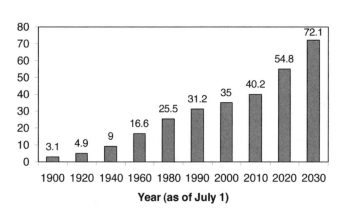

Source: A Profile of Older Americans: 2006 Administration on Aging, U.S. Department of Health and Human Services

The concept behind Social Security was a simple, and brilliant one: have today's workers pay for today's retirees. Then, when today's workers reach retirement age themselves, a new generation of workers will in turn foot the bill for them. That works fine as long as each succeeding generation is larger than the one before it (so that there are enough workers paying into the system each year to support the number of retirees).

But the whole house of cards falls apart when there is a spurt of population growth, followed by a sharp decline. In that case, there simply aren't enough workers to support the disproportionately large number of retirees. And things get worse still when people live longer, as they do today—much longer, in fact, then people did back in 1935 when Social Security was introduced and benefits were expected to be paid out for only a few years on average.

Sadly, that's exactly the desperate situation we find ourselves in today.

DEMOGRAPHICS 101

They say a picture is worth a thousand words, so let's take a look at a few illustrations taken from the U.S. government census report entitled "65+ In The United States," issued in 2005.

Here's a graph showing U.S. population by age and sex at the beginning of the 20th century, in the year 1900:

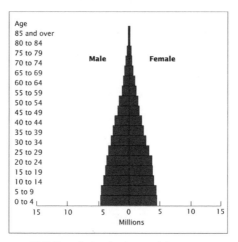

U.S. Population by Age and Sex: 1900

As you can see, the shape resembles a pyramid, meaning that the population was fairly evenly divided between men and women, with more younger people and fewer older people. The graph also shows that most people alive at the time were under the age of 24, with few individuals older than 65 and almost no one above the age of 80. This is indicative of a slowly growing population with a relatively short life span.

Here's how things had changed forty years later:

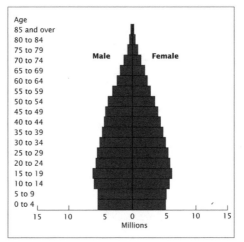

U.S. Population by Age and Sex: 1940

The wider dimensions means that there's been considerable population growth, and it's also apparent that most people alive at that time were between 10 and 40 years of age. (The slight decrease in the number of young children is probably a reflection of the hardships of the Great Depression.) There are also considerably more people in the 65 to 80 age bracket—a reflection of improved health care and better living conditions—and a slight increase in the number of people aged 80 or more.

So far, so good. The trends appear stable and fairly predictable: growth in all age groups, with people starting to live a bit longer.

The big surprise comes when we take a look at the U.S. population in 1960, as shown in the graph on the following page.

See that big base in gray at the bottom of the pyramid? That's the "baby boom" generation—people born between 1946

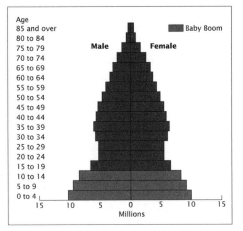

U.S. Population by Age and Sex: 1960

and 1964. In total, there were 78 million new births during that period, 76 million of whom were born here and another 2 million immigrants of baby boomer age.[17] In 1960, these newly minted Americans accounted for almost a quarter of the total population;[18] even today, despite the fact that there have been nearly 50 years worth of new births (and despite the fact that our elderly are living longer), they still account for some 28 percent of the total U.S. population.[19]

Why this massive—and thoroughly unprecedented—spike? The primary explanation lies in the fact that millions of soldiers had just returned home from fighting World War II. Relieved to have survived and to be back on American soil, their main goal was to meet a girl, fall in love, marry, and raise a family.

Another huge factor was the rapid expansion of the American economy during the postwar years. The mobilization towards war accounted for part of that—whole new industries sprang up, fattened by huge government contracts, with women contributing significantly to the labor force for the first time in this country's history. In addition, because many of the factories in Europe and Japan had been bombed out, the U.S. became the main source for pretty much every kind of manufactured goods. (Interestingly, the only other three major industrialized nations that hadn't been bombed during World War II—Canada, Australia, and New Zealand—all experienced sustained postwar baby booms as well.[20])

For people who had lived through the Great Depression and then faced the horrors of war, the promise of the postwar years was almost too good to be true. Optimism reigned supreme, giving rise to the so-called "American Dream"—a house, a car, a loving spouse, a well-paying, secure job, and money in the bank. And, of course, children.

Given the benefit of hindsight, one could almost make a case that people went a little overboard on the children front at that time: 92 percent of all women who could have children did.[21] During the baby boom years, there was an average of 3.8 kids per household,[22] leading unfortunately to the overcrowding of roads, schools, and cities that we all face today.

And, more than any previous generation, baby boomer children were indulged—some might even say spoiled—because their parents were flush and didn't want to deprive their offspring of anything. As a result, the baby boomer generation hasn't been good about saving—certainly not nearly as good as the previous generation that had lived through traumatic events like depression and war and thus knew the value of saving for a rainy day. Boomers tend to be financial optimists because in their childhood they had everything and felt that everything was possible. There was a prevailing feeling of what the politicians and ad executives of the time called "freedom from want," and the consumer-driven society of the late 1940s, 1950s, and early 1960s capitalized on it mercilessly. As a result, there soon sprang up a culture of debt, created almost entirely by the baby boomers. It's worth noting that there was little household debt before the boomer generation, and no credit cards: people paid as they went, and if you couldn't afford something, you simply didn't buy it. Boomers, in contrast, tend to buy pretty much whatever they want even if it means borrowing money to pay for it. In 1946, average consumer debt was 22 percent of the annual household income.[23] Today, it's a quite frightening 120 percent of household income.[24]

Baby boomers are about to become the largest and longest-lived generation in American history. Whether that's good news or bad news depends on your point of view. If you're a boomer who's counting on Social Security and other government entitlements, it's *really* bad news, as you'll soon see.

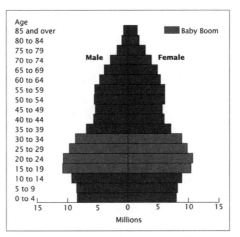

U.S. Population by Age and Sex: 1980

This graph shows the state of U.S. population in 1980. The boomer generation—the bulge in the middle representing people in their teens, twenties, and early thirties—continues to stick out like the proverbial sore thumb. It's even more obvious because, from 1964 to 1980, there was a significant *decline* in the number of births. That's partly because of the impact of the birth control pill and partly because it was a time when many American women pursued careers and so decided to wait before they had children. There were other cultural considerations which made having families a lower priority, plus a lot of single women began adopting children—something which became not just acceptable in society, but fashionable. During that period, only about 3 - 3.5 million of these "Generation X" babies were born each year, as opposed to the 4 million or so that were born each year during the baby boom era.[25]

Here's how things had changed by the beginning of the 21st century:

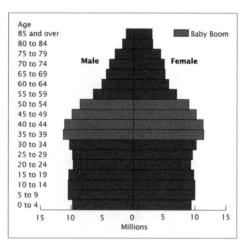

U.S. Population by Age and Sex: 2000

As you can see, the baby boomer generation—now aging into their forties and fifties—continues to create a bulge despite a modest increase in population during the 1980s and early 1990s. This increase occurred for a number of reasons, including the fact that the women who had decided to wait to have children back in the 1960s and 1970s realized that they were starting to run out of time. Many of them also began to hit the so-called "glass ceiling" and realized their careers couldn't progress much further. In addition, the Reagan era gave rise to a new resurgence of family values and a return to the promise of the American dream. The population born in this era are known as the "Echo Boom"—the children of baby boomers. Again, it's worth noting that this didn't occur right after the baby boom—there was a period in-between of some twenty years.

Now let's take a look at the U.S. census population projections for the years 2020 and 2040, based on current trends:

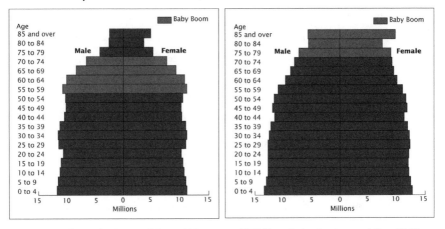

U.S. Population by Age and Sex: 2020   U.S. Population by Age and Sex: 2040

By the year 2020, America will be on the brink of an elderly boom, and these projections illustrate its magnitude. Since the 1940s, the number of people aged 65 and up has been growing gradually, but that number will increase sharply starting in 2011, as the baby-boom generation begins to turn 65.[26] Today, approximately one out of every eight Americans is 65 or older. By 2030, when the entire baby-boom generation has reached that age, roughly one out of every five Americans will be 65 or older [27]... meaning that the nation as a whole will have a higher percentage of elderly than Florida does today. As in most countries, there are more older women than older men in the United States—a disproportion that increases with age. According to one recent survey, our 65-and-older population is comprised of 58 percent women and 42 percent men. In contrast, the 85-and-older population consists of 70 percent women and only 30 percent men.[28]

Given the decrease in population following the baby boom and the increase in longevity brought about by medical advances, it should come as no surprise that the fastest growing segment of the United States population is in fact the oldest old: that is, people age 85 and up.[29] There are currently more than 4 million of our most senior citizens—nearly twice the 1980 level.[30] But beginning in 2031, when the first baby boomers start reaching the age of 85, that number will start to increase rapidly. Experts predict that there will be a staggering 19 million people over the age of 85 by the year 2050, at which point they will comprise almost 5 percent of the total U.S. population.[31]

There are even projections about centenarians—people age 100 or older. In the year 2000, there were only about 65,000 of these long-lived individuals in the U.S., but even that rarified segment of the population is expected to grow quickly in the coming years; there may be as many as 381,000 centenarians by 2030.[32] The size of this age group will have particular impact on the future of our health care system, because these individuals tend to be in poorer health and require more services than the younger old. But research on the demographics of centenarians, along with clinical, biomedical, and genetic measures, is especially important because it may provide clues to the factors associated with exceptional longevity.

Worldwide, the trends are much the same, though accelerated.

World population has more than doubled in the past 50 years, and has nearly quadrupled since 1900.[33] And people are living longer everywhere, not just in the U.S.—in fact, in some countries, men can expect to live to nearly 80, and women to more than 86.[34] As a result, total global population is comprised of a higher percentage of older people, a trend shown in the graph below[35] that is expected to continue. A recent study conducted by AARP indicated that by 2016, some 39 percent of the total population of the most developed countries will consist of people age 50 and older, up from 30 percent in 2006.

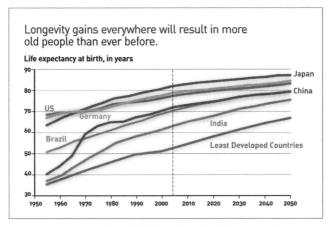

Source: Hayutin, Adele, PhD. from Stanford Center on Longevity,
The Big Picture of Population Change, **2007.**

What's more, in almost every developed country (and even some less developed ones), people are having fewer children, as shown in the graph on the following page. As each country's standard of living goes up, the average number of children per family goes down, because there's less need to have lots of kids to work alongside their parents and take care of them in their old age. This is borne out by UN statistics, which show that average fertility levels in all but the least developed countries dropped from over 5.9 children per woman in the 1970s to about 3.9 children per woman in the 1990s. These numbers are even lower in the so-called "G7" countries (the U.S., Canada, France, Germany, Italy, Japan, and the UK), where fertility rates have plummeted.

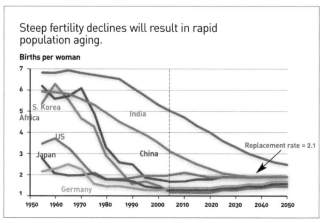

Source: Hayutin, Adele, PhD. from Stanford Center on Longevity, *The Big Picture of Population Change*, 2007.

As a result of these factors, total global population will begin to stabilize or even start to decrease after the next few decades. Today, there are just a handful of developed countries where the population is replacing itself through new births (as opposed to immigration)—the U.S. among them. It's mainly in the sub-Saharan area of Africa and other undeveloped countries where fertility rates are up (although, due to the HIV/AIDS epidemic, life expectancy is much shorter); almost everywhere else, they are down. Even in predominantly Catholic countries (where birth control largely doesn't exist), the numbers have been going down: just 1.2 children per couple were reported in the year 2000 in Italy and Spain. China is an exception. The one-child policy in that country was put into effect years ago because of the famine the country was suffering through, but today, in most rural areas, the rule is ignored. They've relaxed enforcement because of the country's alarming demographics: there are 145 million senior citizens in China (projected to reach 400 million by the year 2051), and one child alone can't take care of two parents, especially since many of them have moved away to the industrial areas of eastern China. Unfortunately, because there are few private charitable organizations to provide supplemental services, the full responsibility is falling on the Chinese government, which, despite offering a limited social social security system, simply doesn't have the money to support all those retirees.

But let's get back to the problem at hand: How are American baby boomers entering their retirement years going to be able to survive financially? Their parents had large families and plenty of children to look after them in old age. However, baby boomers have had fewer kids, have married less often, and have been more likely to live alone. Who will look out for them in their old age?

If you think it will be Uncle Sam, you're wrong. And now that you have a basic understanding of the demographics of population, it will become clear why both Social Security and Medicare (at least in their present form) are in deep, deep trouble.

SOCIAL SECURITY AND MEDICARE: TWO ENDANGERED SPECIES

The simple fact of the matter is that neither Social Security nor Medicare were designed to match the extended size and longevity of the baby boom generation. This should come as no surprise when you consider that Social Security was introduced long before the first baby boomer was born, and that Medicare came into being just before the unexpected decline in population that occurred with the "Generation X" and "Echo Boom" generations of the 1970s and beyond.

When Social Security began back in 1935, there were 32 workers per recipient—that is, 32 people to support every beneficiary. Today there are 3.4 workers per recipient. By the year 2046, there will be less than two workers per recipient.[46] This is not just disturbing news, it's alarming. Our government knows it, too, though so far they have been very slow to react. A 2005 report by the Social Security Administration's own Board of Trustees stated that the SSA trust fund will be exhausted by 2041 if no changes are made to the current law.[47] The trustees also projected that the cost of paying benefits will exceed tax revenue from current workers by 2017, at which point the principal of the trust fund will start to be drawn down.[48] If the trust fund is exhausted, taxes collected will be sufficient to pay only some 70 percent of current-level benefits by the year 2042 (according to the Social Security Administration) or 2052 (according to the Congressional Budget Office's somewhat more optimistic projection).[49]

Similarly, Medicare's Board of Trustees recently predicted that the trust fund that supports Medicare will be exhausted by the year 2019.[50] As we've seen, the percentage of people eligible for Medicare benefits—that is, the population age 65 and over—has risen precipitously over the last few decades and will continue to do so, at least until the last baby boomer reaches eligibility age in 2029. In fact, the Social Security administration itself has estimated that between now and 2027, more than 10,000 Americans *per day* will become eligible for benefits.[51]

We can better understand this grim news if we take a look at something called the "dependency ratio"—a ratio indexing people under the age of 15 and over 64 (who are presumed to be non-wage earners) against the rest of the population (who are presumed to be wage earners). Today the dependency ratio is around 20 (meaning that approximately 20 percent of all Americans are not earning a wage)[52] and barring unforeseen circumstances, this figure should remain stable for another few years. But as baby boomers age, this number is expected to skyrocket to between 30 and 35 by the year 2030,[53] meaning that approximately a third of our total population will be dependent, either on their parents or on government entitlements like Social Security.

It won't have to get that high for the entire system to collapse. Most experts agree that unless there are substantial changes (in the form of higher taxes, lower benefits, older eligibility ages, or all of the above) in the next few years, disaster looms. Already, the age of eligibility has been raised. Baby boomers can only claim full Social Security benefits at age 66 (if they were born before 1960) or 67 (if they were born after 1960)—not 65. According to the Center for Retirement Research at Boston College, "this translates into lower benefits relative to pre-retirement income at any age. In addition, benefits relative to pre-retirement earnings have declined because more wives are working. This outcome is virtually inevitable in a system that provides a 50-percent spouse's benefit. As women go to work, they increase the family's pre-retirement earnings but often fail to increase the couple's Social Security benefit in retirement."[54]

You won't necessarily need to replace 100 percent of your pre-retirement income after you stop working in order to be secure: in fact, most people need between 65 to 85 percent to maintain their standard of living.[55] But today, Social Security just replaces 42 percent of an average worker's earnings[56] (something statisticians call the "replacement rate"). That's bad enough, but even after adjusting for the rising normal retirement age, taxation of benefits, and higher Medicare premiums, experts predict that the net replacement rate will drop to a mere 30 percent by 2030[57]... and that's without factoring in the inevitability of inflation.

"Okay," you may be saying, "I get it. I understand that I can't count on either Social Security or Medicare to take care of my needs after I retire. Good thing I have a company pension and an IRA!"

Oops. Think again.

SHAKY FOUNDATIONS

Employer-sponsored pension plans used to be a significant source of retirement income for the nation's workforce. Most workers remained with their employer until retirement age, after which they would collect their pension (usually based on their final salary and the number of years they had been employed) as well as Social Security benefits. These kinds of plans, combined with the lure of government money in the form of Social Security, tended to discourage workers from remaining on the job past specified target ages. Indeed, it was an important personnel policy objective in many companies to see that workers could, and did, retire in an orderly fashion.

But today traditional pension plans have gone the way of the dodo bird. The decline of the stock market since 1999, combined with corporate greed and fraud (*a la* Enron), has served to hugely deflate the value of such plans. Dr. Robert N. Butler reported that the White House Conference on Aging in 1995 came up with the following summary of the attitude of the private sector today:

(1) We can't promise you how long we'll be in business.

(2) We can't promise you that we won't be bought by another company.

(3) We can't promise that there will be room for promotion.

(4) We can't promise that your job will exist until you reach retirement age.

(5) We can't promise that the money will be available for your pension.

(6) We can't expect your undying loyalty.

And (7) we aren't sure we want it.[58]

The inescapable fact is that a growing number of companies have had to freeze or drastically reduce their traditional pensions and so retirees have been forced to rely on them less and less. In 2003, only 10 percent of all private-sector workers with pensions were covered solely with a defined-benefit plan.[59]

Today's baby boomers have to rely instead on employer-sponsored (and occasionally employer-matched) 401(k) plans as well as self-funded Individual Retirement Account (IRA) plans. But for a variety of reasons (an overriding philosophy of "living for today," combined with a pervading sense of entitlement and the inevitable fiscal irresponsibility that comes from being doted on in their youth), baby boomers have failed to accumulate substantial 401(k) and IRA funds. According to the Center for Retirement Research, the median 401(k) balance for those now approaching retirement age is a paltry $60,000,[60] which translates into an even more paltry income of less than $400 per month.[61]

Even if you're a homeowner, there are no easy solutions. If you think you'll be able to convert the equity in your home into an income stream, you may be in for a nasty surprise. Yes, you can take a reverse mortgage (where the mortgage holder pays you a monthly income and promises not to ever evict you... in exchange for hefty fees and the deed to your house), but you'll find that you can only tap a portion of your home's value: about 45 percent at current interest rates, and less if rates rise from today's low levels.[62]

And even if you have assets and investments, the reality is that nobody expects them to perform in the next twenty years like they did in the last twenty years—they almost certainly won't go up at the same rate and may not even go up at all, after accounting for inflation. Inflation is a killer, especially if you're living on a fixed income. In the 1970s, prices rose, on average, about 7 percent a year.[63] For the past several years, it's been hovering around 3 percent, [64] but if the annual rate were to rise to the 4 or 5 percent of the late 1980s (or, worse yet, the 10 to 13 percent of the early 80s), purchasing power would take a jolt and it would have a significant impact on fixed-income portfolios. So all indications are that the share of earnings replaced at any given age by Social Security and both employer and individual retirement plans will be less; even worse, that income stream will also be less secure than it ever has in the past.

To be blunt, it all adds up to a pretty grim picture...but certainly not a hopeless one. Plan ahead and I assure you that you can not only *survive* retirement, but *thrive* in your retirement, both financially and emotionally. And as you do your planning, remember that it's important to be realistic, but equally important to be optimistic. As the 19th century journalist William Allen White once wrote, "I am not afraid of tomorrow because I have seen yesterday and I love today."

Those, my friends, are truly words to live by.

Endnotes

[1] *Life Tables for Males*, 1900-2030,U.S. Social Security Administration

[2] Ibid

[3] PBS documentary, "The Boomer Century: 1946-2046"

[4] op. cit., *Life Tables for Males*, 1900-2030

[5] *65+ In The United States: 2005*, National Institute on Aging / U.S. Census Bureau

[6] American Academy of Actuaries

[7] Scommegna, Paola, *U.S. Growing Bigger, Older, and More Diverse*, Population Reference Bureau, http://www.prb.org/Articles/2004/ USGrowingBiggerOlderandMoreDiverse.aspx

[8] Manton, Gu and Lamb, *National Long-Term Care Survey (NLTCS), 1984-2004/2005*, Duke University, 2006

[9] *McKinsey 2006 Consumer Retirement Survey*, Congressional Research Service

[10] *Survey of 1,000 Americans Over 45*, Aetna and the Financial Planning Association

[11] TIAA-CREF Management Group

[12] *Frequently Asked Questions: Age 65 Retirement*, U.S. Government Social Security Online, http://www.ssa.gov/history/age65.html

[13] Ibid

[14] PBS documentary, "The Boomer Century: 1946-2046"

[15] National Center for Health Statistics, *National Vital Statistics Reports*, vol. 54, no. 19

[16] *A Profile of Older Americans: 2006*, Administration on Aging, U.S. Department of Health and Human Services

[17] op.cit., "The Boomer Century: 1946-2046"

[18] *Population Distribution by Age, Race, Nativity, and Sex Ratio, 1860–2005*, InfoPlease U.S. Statistics, http://www.infoplease.com/ipa/A0110384.html

[19] *Baby Boomer Facts*, 50 Plus Central, http://www.50pluscentral.com/ Baby%20Boomer%20Facts.htm

[20] *Population: The Industrialized Nations Since 1950*, Encyclopædia Britannica Online, 2007, http://www.britannica.com/eb/article-60689

WHEN I'M 64

[21] op.cit., "The Boomer Century: 1946-2046"

[22] Ibid

[23] Ibid, and *Flow of Funds*, Board of Governors of the Federal Reserve System.

[24] op.cit., "The Boomer Century: 1946-2046"

[25] *Live Births and Birth Rates, by Year*, InfoPlease U.S. Statistics, http://www.infoplease.com/ipa/A0005067.html

[26] op. cit., 65+ In The United States: 2005

[27] Ibid

[28] *Population 2000*, Federal Interagency Forum on Aging-Related Statistics, http://www.agingstats.gov/agingstatsdotnet/Main_Site/Data/2000_Documents/Population.pdf

[29] Ibid

[30] *Older Americans Update 2006*, Federal Interagency Forum on Aging Related Statistics, 2006, http://www.agingstats.gov/agingstatsdotnet/Main_Site/Data/2006_Documents/OA_2006.pdf

[31] op. cit., *65+ In The United States: 2005*

[32] op. cit., *Population 2000*

[33] *The World at Six Billion*, United Nations, http://www.un.org/esa/population/publications/sixbillion/sixbilpart1.pdf

[34] op. cit., *AARP Profit From Experience*

[35] Hayutin, Adele, PhD, *The Big Picture of Population Change*, Stanford Center on Longevity, 2007

[36] op. cit., *AARP Profit From Experience*

[37] op. cit., *The Big Picture of Population Change*

[38] *World Fertility Report 2003*, United Nations, http://www.un.org/esa/population/publications/worldfertility/World_Fertility_Report.htm

[39] op. cit., *AARP Profit From Experience*

[40] *World Population to 2300*, United Nations, http://www.un.org/esa/population/publications/longrange2/WorldPop2300final.pdf

[41] Ibid

[42] Connell, Christopher, *Getting Old Fast*, Stanford Medicine, Spring 2008

[43] op.cit., *World Population to 2300*, United Nations

[44] Ibid

[45] China National Committee on Aging, 2006

[46] op.cit., "The Boomer Century: 1946-2046"

[47] *2007 Annual Reports*, Social Security and Medicare Boards of Trustees, http://www.ssa.gov/OACT/TRSUM/

[48] Ibid

[49] op. cit., Eisenberg, 66

[50] op. cit., *Annual Reports*

[51] *Nation's First Baby Boomer Files for Social Security Retirement Benefits Online*, Social Security Administration news release, October 15, 2007

[52] *Census Bureau-Projected Dependency Ratios, 2000-2100*, 2000

[53] Ibid

[54] Munnell, Sass, and Aubry, *Employer Survey: 1 Out of 4 Boomers Won't Retire Because They Can't*, Center for Retirement Research at Boston College, Series 6, December 2006

[55] *Myths and Realities About Retirement Preparedness*, Center for Retirement Research at Boston College, May 2006

[56] *2004 Social Security Trustees Report*, U.S. Social Security Administration, 2004

[57] Munnell, Buessing, Soto, and Sass, *Will We Have To Work Forever?*, Center for Retirement Research at Boston College, July 2006

[58] Letter to Aging Today, January 2007

[59] op. cit., *Myths and Realities About Retirement Preparedness*

[60] Munnell and Sunden, 401(k) *Plans Are Still Coming Up Short*, Center for Retirement Research at Boston College, March 2006

[61] Ibid

[62] op. cit., *Myths and Realities About Retirement Preparedness*

[63] *Historical U.S. Inflation Rate 1914 - Present*, InflationData.com, http://inflationdata.com/inflation/Inflation_Rate/HistoricalInflation.aspx

[64] Ibid

BIBLIOGRAPHY

50 Plus Central, *Baby Boomer Facts*

Aetna and the Financial Planning Association, *Survey of 1,000 Americans Over 45*

Butler, Dr. Robert N., *Why Survive? Being Old In America*, The Johns Hopkins University Press, 2002

Butler, Dr. Robert N., *The Longevity Revolution: The Benefits and Challenges of Living a Long Life*, PublicAffairs, 2008

Center for Retirement Research at Boston College, *Myths and Realities About Retirement Preparedness*, May 2006

Cohen, Gene, *The Mature Mind: The Positive Power of the Aging Brain*, Basic Books, 2007

Congressional Research Service, *McKinsey 2006 Consumer Retirement Survey*, 2006

Eisenberg, Lee, *The Number*, Free Press, 2006

Encyclopædia Britannica Online, *Population: The Industrialized Nations Since 1950*, 2007

Erikson, Erik, *Childhood and Society*, Norton, 1950

Federal Interagency Forum on Aging Related Statistics, *Older Americans Update 2006*, 2006

Federal Interagency Forum on Aging-Related Statistics, *Population 2000*

Gladwell, Malcolm, *The Tipping Point*, Back Bay Books, 2002

Hayutin, Adele, Ph.D, *The Big Picture of Population Change*, Stanford Center on Longevity, 2007

InfoPlease U.S. Statistics, *Live Births and Birth Rates, by Year*

InfoPlease U.S. Statistics, *Population Distribution by Age, Race, Nativity, and Sex Ratio, 1860–2005*

Johnson, Spencer, *Who Moved My Cheese?*, Putnam Adult, 1998

Levitan, Dan, *This Is Your Brain On Music*, Dutton, 2006

Manton, Gu and Lamb, *National Long-Term Care Survey (NLTCS), 1984-2004/2005*, Duke University, 2006

Munnell and Sunden, *401(k) Plans Are Still Coming Up Short*, Center for Retirement Research at Boston College, March 2006

Munnell, Buessing, Soto, and Sass, *Will We Have To Work Forever?*, Center for Retirement Research at Boston College, July 2006

Munnell, Sass, and Aubry, *Employer Survey: 1 Out of 4 Boomers Won't Retire Because They Can't*, Center for Retirement Research at Boston College, Series 6, December 2006

National Center for Health Statistics, *National Vital Statistics Reports*, vol. 54, no. 19

National Institute on Aging / U.S. Census Bureau, *65+ In The United States: 2005*

Nuland, Sherwin, *The Art of Aging*, Random House, 2007

Scommegna, Paola, *U.S. Growing Bigger, Older, and More Diverse*, Population Reference Bureau

Social Security and Medicare Boards of Trustees, *2007 Annual Reports*

Sugarman, Joseph, *Advertising Secrets of the Written Word*, Delstar Publications, 1998

U.S. Government Social Security Online, *Frequently Asked Questions: Age 65 Retirement*

U.S. Social Security Administration, *2004 Social Security Trustees Report*

U.S. Social Security Administration, *Life Tables for Males, 1900-2030*

United Nations Publications, *The World at Six Billion*

United Nations Publications, *World Fertility Report 2003*

United Nations Publications, *World Population to 2300*

Wind, Crook, and Gunther, Robert, *The Power of Impossible Thinking*, Wharton School Publishing, 2004

Wolfe, David, and Snyder, Robert, *Ageless Marketing*, Kaplan Business, 2003

World Health Organization (WHO), *Health and Aging— A Discussion Paper*, 2002

RESOURCES

Elderhostel
www.elderhostel.org

University of the Third Age
www.u3aonline.org

HEALTH

Alzheimer's Association
www.alz.org

Posit Science Corporation
www.positscience.com

Memory Fitness Matters
www.memoryfitnessmatters.com

EMPLOYMENT

Civic Ventures
www.civicventures.org

Monster.com
http://content.monster.com/GetTheJob/factor/3/home.aspx

Retired Brains
www.retiredbrains.com

Senior Job Bank
www.seniorjobbank.org

YourEncore
www.yourencore.com

VOLUNTEERING

AmeriCorps
www.americorps.gov

Executive Service Corps
www.escus.org

Experience Corps
www.experiencecorps.org

Habitat for Humanity
www.habitat.org

Mentor
www.mentoring.org

Peace Corps
www.peacecorps.gov

Senior Corps
www.seniorcorps.org

USA Freedom Corps
www.usafreedomcorps.gov

Creative Discovery Corps
http://www.gwumc.edu/cahh/discover/index.htm

Volunteers In Medicine Institute
www.vimi.org

RETIREMENT ADVOCATES

American Association of Retired Persons
www.aarp.org

American Society on Aging
833 Market Street, Suite 511
San Francisco, CA 94103
(415) 974-9600
(800) 537-9728
www.asaging.org

2young2retire
www.2young2retire.com

MOTIVATIONAL SPEAKING AND LECTURE ORGANIZATIONS

Marvin Tolkin is available for lectures and motivational
speaking. For more information, visit www.marvintolkin.com

ACKNOWLEDGEMENTS

IN MANY WAYS, *When I'm 64* is the story of my life. There have been so many important people who have had such a profound influence on me throughout the years, and I'd like to express my heartfelt gratitude to all of them.

First and foremost, I want to thank the two most important women in my life: Carole and Estelle. My lovely bride Carole means the world to me. She opened the door to my new life just at a time when I was casting around for purpose. Estelle, too, was always there for me, and she always provided unequivocal support and devotion to me and to our family. It was her total confidence in me that gave me the opportunity to take risks and make all the different kinds of investments detailed in these pages.

I worked alongside my loving father, Irving Tolkin, for more than twenty years. He taught me everything he knew, and then he let me do it. He led our family from darkness into light, and that light gave me focus and the self-confidence to go forward. He also gave me the ultimate gift: the gift of planning.

From my mother Isabel Tolkin, I learned risk tolerance. She was a card player, and even when she was 91 years old, I could never beat her at gin rummy! She had such an adventurous spirit, and she was was as smart as a whip, too. It was a combination of the determination I got from my father and my mother's willingness to take risks that allowed me to formulate the retirement plan that I continue to enjoy to this very day.

I was actually fortunate enough to have two fathers, if you count my father-in-law Bob Judelson, a very special man who always treated me like a son. He had an indomitable spirit, and if I could have bottled it, I could have sold it for $10,000 a pop! He knew how to take adversity and not only overcome it but change it into love. I have so many warm memories of Bob and his sweet wife, Hannah, and I will never forget them.

As much as I learned in the business world, I owe as least as much to the education I got from watching my three sons grow up into the fine adults they are today. I love them all dearly and admire each of them for their own individual traits: Steven, for his independence and pioneering spirit; Larry, who is the best negotiator I know; and David, for his keen, analytical mind.

Then there are all my step-children and sons- and daughters-in-law: Betty, Jacquie, Linda, Stacey, Bob, Melissa, Bill, David, and Orli, and my amazing grandchildren: Alex, Ben, Emma, Kyle, Liza, Elliot, Miles, Jeremiah, Daniel, Leah, Austen, Kaitlyn, Noa, and Maya, the newest member of our family. I'd also like to thank my brothers Sam and Arnold, and Arnold's wife Barbara. Through thick and thin, good times and bad, Sam and Arnold have always been there for me, and their talent has always shone through. I'd like to acknowledge Estelle's brother Jerry, his wife Elaine and their children Bruce and Richard; all my other nephews and my niece Jennifer Dale, for whom I named my company; and Carole's mother Doris and her aunts Gertie, Ruth, and the always outrageous Phyllis. Micha and Suzy Raber started out as business acquaintances but became close friends and are now very much part of my extended family. And I'd be remiss if I didn't mention my favorite aunt and uncle: Celia and Jack Press. Uncle Jack started it all with that Irish Sweepstakes ticket! He was a wonderful man...and the best handball player I've ever seen.

Special thanks to my co-author Howard Massey for skillfully capturing my voice in the pages of this book, and for guiding *When I'm 64* from its initial concept to finished product. Heartfelt appreciation also to Dr. Robert N. Butler for his gracious and articulate Foreword, and to Lee Eisenberg, who gave me the inspiration to write this book. Special thanks also to author Adriane Berg and to markerting experts David Wolfe and Dick Ambrosius and the members of their organization, The Society. I am grateful to Dr. Adele Hayutin of the Stanford Center on Longevity for her kind permission to use some of her research materials here; to Lani Adler and Eric Prager for their legal vetting; and to Sherry Williams at Oxygen Design for her beautiful graphic design of this book.

My many years running Jennifer Dale were challenging and at times hectic, but equally rewarding and pleasurable, thanks to the many great people we had working there. I'd like to single out my business partners Morris Yohai, Lenny Roberto, Ron Frank, and Burt Rosenberg for special mention; we were like brothers, and there was a camaraderie and trust between us that was priceless. There was nothing Morris wouldn't do for the company—he used to stay late at night, working on making patterns. Lenny could do any job at the plant: he opened it in the morning and closed it at night. Ron was a super-salesman who could sell snowballs to Eskimos. And Burt was an inventive thinker who guided me in the company's initial financial planning. I'd like to give a special mention also to Odelle Berkowitz and Sal Falonga, and to our key designers: Carol Lindberg, Cheryl Leggi, Jeanne Fauci, and Mary Ellen Markowitz. Each had their own touch, but they all had remarkable ability, and it was their composite talent that was such an integral part of Jennifer Dale's success. I'd also like to thank the sales staff, who taught me how to sell, especially Eddie Bryce and Al Stockbower, and all the store buyers, who took in a young kid and made him a pro.

I'd like to express my appreciation to Bernie Davis, who taught me that stress is nothing to be afraid of, because stress, challenge, and risk are all tied together, and to our longtime accountant Sol Bergstein. Sol was a no-nonsense guy who had an uncanny ability to look at any situation and tell you exactly what was right about it, and what was wrong about it. I should have listened to him more often! Gerry Marsden was another excellent thinker who took over after Sol's passing, and Arthur Andreucci became a dear friend who I could always count on to bring me back down to earth whenever my ideas started getting a little too high-flying. In addition, I'd like to thank Leon Jaffe, our first attorney, who showed me what a really smart lawyer could accomplish.

In my current career, I'd like to offer special thanks to Igal Jellinek, executive director of the Council of Senior Centers and Services of New York City, for whom I serve as business consultant. He welcomed me into the community with open arms and has brought new purpose to my life. I'd also like to express my appreciation to Rabbi Stanley Platek and his wife Cele, not only for his spiritual guidance, but for their friendship, and to Alex Alexandrov, for showing me that the American dream is still alive and well. Last but not least, thanks to Yvette and Victor Hershaft, Steve Murphy, Ted O'Lear, Mark Kazmac, David Weber, Kevin Blackburn, Don Hendel, and Gene Kline.

Howard Massey would like to thank his Ideal Reader, Deborah Gremito, for her advice, patience, and loving support, as well as Kathy and Brian Games, Matthew Games, Steve Parr, Sharon Rose-Parr, Peter Fields, Scott Anderson, Vernon Benjamin, Miriam Ben-Yaacov, Jeff Moody, Jo Salas, Violet Snow, Rachel Weissman, and Minda Zetlin.

GIVE THE GIFT THAT KEEPS ON GIVING!

Share the stories, wisdom, and practical advice of
When I'm 64: Planning for the Best of Your Life
with family, friends, and colleagues

Order your copies today!

Use the coupon below or visit
www.whenim64.com

Special offer: buy four copies,
get one free (pay only S/H).*

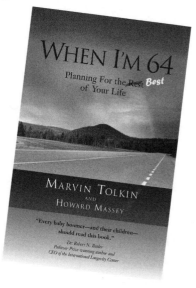

* Offer expires 12/31/09

- -

Yes! I'd like to order _____ copies of *When I'm 64: Planning for the Best of Your Life* at $14.95 each, plus $4.95 shipping and handling for each book.

Name _____

Address _____

City _____ State _____ Zip _____

I enclose check or money order in the amount of $ _____

Mail to: Tributary Press
          132 East 35 Street #8C
          New York, NY 10016

For credit card orders, please visit our website at
www.whenim64.com